Psychological Courage

Daniel Putman

UNIVERSITY PRESS OF AMERICA,® INC.
Dallas • Lanham • Boulder • New York • Oxford

Library of Congress Control Number: 2004100975
ISBN 0-7618-2820-6 (clothbound : alk. ppr.)
ISBN 0-7618-2821-4 (paperback : alk. ppr.)

Contents

Acknowledgments

To my colleagues in the UW Colleges Philosophy Department and Marc Potash and Michael O'Brien, all of whom helped me develop and sort through ideas in the book. And to Kathy Skubal, without whose practical help over the years this book would not exist.

Prologue

THE THREE FORMS OF COURAGE

In 1998, Timmy Stackpole of Ladder Company 103 tumbled through a collapsing floor in a burning building. He survived—just barely. Over 30 percent of his body was burned; bone could be seen through melted flesh. "I had big, big doubts he would make it," says Msgr. Thomas Brady, pastor of the Roman Catholic Church of the Good Shepherd, where Stackpole and his wife, Tara, were parishioners.

The father of five refused to give up. Two months later, he walked out of the hospital, still bandaged but wearing his trademark smile. This March, after a long rehab, he was back on the job at last.

Everything seemed perfect for Stackpole, Tara, and their kids, ages 6 to 18. He had recently earned a business degree and was promoted to captain a few weeks ago. But on September 11, the Stackpoles' world was again shaken.

Tara, 37, was visiting her mother when she heard about the attack on the World Trade Center. "I know he's there," she would tell Monsignor Brady later. Her hunch was right.

For a week, they clung to any flicker of light. "If anybody could make it out, we knew Timmy could," said family friend Nancy Falco as she waited at Good Shepherd School last Tuesday to pick up her son and 10-year-old Brian Stackpole. Minutes later, Monsignor Brady would leave the rectory for Tara and Timmy's little blue-and-white-shingled semidetached house on East 37th Street, in a working-class, Irish-Italian Catholic enclave in the shadow of Coney Island. He had news: Timmy, 42, had been found in the wreckage of the World Trade Center. They say firefighters from another unit found his body but stepped aside to let his New York City brethren pull him out.

By Thursday, daughter Kaitlin's 15th birthday, everyone in the close-knit neighborhood knew. Visitors streamed in and out of the Stackpole house. "There is great emptiness," says Falco. "We held out hope until the very last minute. But Tara knows he did what he had to do. He's one of the heroes of the 21st century."

U.S. News & World Report, October 1, 2001

When he noticed that a white person had to stand, the bus driver, James F. Blake, called out to the four black people who were sitting just behind the white section. He said they would have to give up their seats for the new passenger. No one stood up. "You'd better make it light on yourself and let me have those seats," the driver said threateningly. Three men got up and went to stand at the back of the bus. But Rosa Parks wasn't about to move. She had been in this situation before, and she had always given up her seat. She had always felt insulted by the experience. "It meant that I didn't have a right to do anything but get on the bus, give them my fare and then be pushed around wherever they wanted me," she said.

By a quirk of fate, the driver of the bus on this December evening was the same James F. Blake who had once before removed the troublesome Rosa Parks from his bus for refusing to enter by the back door. That was a long time ago, in 1943. Rosa Parks didn't feel like being pushed around again. She told the driver that she wasn't in the white section and she wasn't going to move.

Blake knew the rules, though. He knew that the white section was wherever the driver said it was. If more white passengers got on the bus, he could stretch the white section to the back of the bus and make all the blacks stand. He shouted to Rosa Parks to move to the back of the bus. She wasn't impressed. She told him again that she wasn't moving. Everyone in the bus was silent, wondering what would happen next. Finally Blake told Rosa Parks that he would have her arrested for violating the racial segregation codes. In a firm but quiet voice, she told him that he could do what he wanted to do because she wasn't moving.

"Rosa Parks" by Kai Friese in *The Book of Virtues*,
edited by William Bennett, 290.

Jill is a 25-year-old single woman who works as a flight attendant for a major airline. After getting home late at night after a particularly difficult flight, Jill went out to a local convenience store and bought a half gallon of chocolate ice cream, a 1-pound box of cookies, a medium-sized frozen pizza, a loaf of French bread, and a quart of milk. When she got home, she put the pizza in the oven and waited impatiently for it to cook; everything else stayed on the table. When the pizza was just edible, she brought it out and placed it with the other food. She then lunged into the food and ate everything she bought as quickly as she could, stuffing in huge mouthfuls and dribbling milk, crumbs, and pizza sauce down her chin and on her blouse. When she finished, she ran to the bathroom, knelt in front of the toilet, thrust her hand down her throat, and vomited everything she had just eaten . . .

Before her appointment at the clinic, Jill read several articles about this disorder and was very relieved to find out that, as her internist had said, many other women suffered from these same odd symptoms. When her therapist asked her what brought her to the eating disorders clinic, she looked down and replied, "I have bulimia."

Casebook in Abnormal Psychology, 3rd edition,
edited by John Vitkus, 241–42.

Introduction

The purpose of this book is to explore a particular kind of courage, what I call "psychological courage." I want to support the idea that "courage" is a completely appropriate term for facing our inner fears—our phobias, bad habits, unhealthy psychological relationships. I also want to bring recognition to the millions of people who have had the strength of character to overcome psychological barriers to growth. In the last 100 years a medical understanding of the brain has helped relieve suffering for millions of people. Many conditions thought to be unsolvable can now be treated by appropriate drugs or forms of behavioral therapy. It is easy to lose sight of the difficult psychological decisions many people must make, sometimes on a daily basis. Despite the advances in medicine, people continue to go through powerful personal struggles with their own emotions and habits. They have to make difficult and painful *choices* that have far-reaching ethical implications for themselves, their loved ones, and those with whom they work. This book will examine those choices, especially the role of courage, in the light of modern psychology.

First, however, it is important to distinguish psychological courage from other types of courage. Two other types of courage have been discussed a great deal in history. "Physical courage" is overcoming a fear of death or physical harm. The goals of physical courage are traditionally defined by society or by the requirements of survival. A clear example is the courageous soldier who faces death in war or the firefighters who faced death to save innocent people in the World Trade Center. Another example would be bravely defending your family against a threat from nature such as a flood. In all these examples we admire the courage of the person because he or she chose to risk life for the sake of something greater or larger—country, family or the lives of other people.

The second form is "moral courage." In moral courage the major concern is maintaining ethical integrity or what some philosophers have called "authenticity." In moral courage you fight to keep your integrity while at the same time overcoming the fear of being rejected. Examples are common and are much more likely to be encountered in everyday life than cases of physical courage: confronting your peer group over a racist joke, standing up for someone whose reputation is being smeared by gossip, facing ostracism from colleagues for calling attention to injustice in the workplace. Examples of physical and moral courage often overlap. Gandhi and King exhibited moral courage while at the same time facing death. Though physical and moral courage often go together, the distinction is useful for thinking about different forms of courageous experience. In physical courage the goal is more externally defined—a nation's freedom, another person's life, or your family's safety—and the fear to be overcome is primarily physical—that is, torture, bodily pain or death. In moral courage the goal is more internally defined— a moral principle that may actually go against society or peers—and the fear to be overcome is more social death than physical death, though physical suffering may be involved.

In "psychological courage" the fear to be faced is not usually physical harm nor is loss of moral integrity a major concern. The fear centers around a loss of psychological stability. This is the courage it takes to face our irrational fears and anxieties, those emotions that hold us in bondage. These can range from habits and compulsions to phobias. Why is confronting a phobia or addiction an act of courage? First, as in moral courage, to admit the problem is to face the possibility of being stigmatized by society. Admitting weakness in your public self-image is incredibly difficult, especially when it involves a very personal problem. Second, a great deal of pain, physical and psychological, can be involved in confronting anxiety or changing a habit, and the individual knows this beforehand. Third, and unique to this form of courage, the stability of the mind itself is threatened (or perceived to be threatened) by the process of coping with the problem. Put another way, in psychological courage it is the *psyche itself* whose loss is threatened. The foreboding sense of anxiety that accompanies obsessive-compulsive disorder, or the fear of losing a grip on reality if a drug habit is relinquished, are fears of a kind of psychic death. Courage in the face of psychic death can be as profoundly difficult as courage in the face of physical death.

This book will pull together information from a number of sources in psychology and ethics and examine four aspects of psychological courage. First is the courage needed to admit a mistake, a common everyday experience. I am not talking about a moral mistake necessarily, though that is one form of it. What I am talking about is the admission of a personal failing, especially when society or peers think better of you. Joan is highly regarded in her community and at work but has a secret gambling addiction which she knows is destroying her life. How will she handle her problem? Courage here is closely tied to overcoming self-deception and the book will explore the relationship of courage to the techniques we use to lie to ourselves. Second, beyond being able to admit a weakness, is the courage to face self-generated fears and anxieties. These are fears the outside world would call fantasies or exaggerations but which are very real to the individual. Ben experiences intense anxiety if he is not in total control of a situation. Carrie will not get in a car; she "freezes up" even at the thought of it. Chapter Two will explore the role of courage in dealing with anxiety.

Third, the book will explore the courage to face external psychological threats such as an abusive spouse or manipulative colleagues or parents. Chapter Three will also examine the courage it takes to deal with the pressures social groups put on all of us. Valerie has been in an abusive and manipulative relationship for three years now. Her self-esteem is being crushed and she knows it. What will she do? Jon's Latino neighbor could use some help but the other neighbors would ostracize Jon if he did anything and his self-esteem relies heavily on what others think of him. Can he overcome that fear of what "others will think?" In this example, as in many others, psychological courage and moral courage clearly overlap. Finally, I want to examine the positive and life-fulfilling results of the courage to face reality. While the first three chapters all touch on this, in Chapter Four I want to spell out issues like the courage involved in forming and maintaining a friendship or marriage, the positive effect of psychological courage on society, and the inner peace that virtues like courage can bring to life. Denise's life-long friendship with Jan appears to be ending because Jan is acting in ways Denise thinks are harmful to both of them. What should she do? Married 20 years, David and Marie's marriage has become "routine." Everything seems so smooth yet both feel that life is passing them by. They are afraid to talk about it. Change is risky. Psychological courage is a big issue for them.

A flourishing life with ourselves and with one another depends on the virtues and courage—physical, moral, psychological—is absolutely central in achieving that. Cowardice about our inner fears and anxieties keeps us in a shell and distorts our perception of what is happening in the world around us. Psychological fears blind us and diminish us. For millions of human beings psychological courage is critical in gaining or regaining control of their lives.

Chapter One

The Courage To Admit Weakness

OVERCOMING DESTRUCTIVE HABITS

"I'm Joe, and I'm an alcoholic." "I'm Nancy, and I'm an alcoholic." Cathy looked uneasily around her at the group of strangers in the basement meeting room of the church. She had decided to attend a meeting of Alcoholics Anonymous after seeing a television commercial earlier that week. The first step, it was said, was to admit to oneself that one was an alcoholic. Like many problem drinkers, Cathy had avoided that frightening confrontation for several years, fooling herself with intellectual games such as the proper definition of alcoholism, the scientific status of alcohol as an addicting drug, and other academic questions that protected her from facing the fact that her drinking was out of control and threatening to ruin her life, whether she was actually addicted or not. She recalled from a psychology course in college that AA helped many people stop drinking, so why not her?

"I'm Cathy, and I'm a . . . a . . . ." She stopped in midsentence, looked beseechingly at the upturned face of an older woman sitting in the row in front of her as if to ask this woman what to say next. The stranger smiled and nodded, somehow helping Cathy take what might be her first step to helping herself: ". . . I'm an alcoholic." She marveled to herself how relieved she felt just saying these words aloud, words reflecting a thought she had believed would itself spell ruination. But nothing terrible happened. No one in the room laughed, no one cried. They just greeted her by name, and the meeting went on as it had been proceeding before she spoke.

> *Case Studies in Abnormal Psychology*, 4th edition,
> edited by Thomas Oltmanns, John Neale and Gerald Davison, 183.

Bad habits are hard to break and the thought of stopping addictive habits like alcoholism can be terrifying. Habits, good and bad, form the core of what we call our "character." So we can talk about John being a patient man or Lisa being a generous woman because "patient man" and "generous woman" refer to habits these two people routinely follow. Likewise, if Ruth is stingy or Richard is cowardly, those traits may also refer to long-standing and deeply entrenched habits — habits traditionally called vices. Of course judging someone else's character is not easy — or at least not easy to do well. But, granted that, it does make sense to say that all of us have certain strong tendencies and habits that form what we call our character.

But a person's character is not set in stone. Harmful habits may have strong roots in our childhood but we are not slaves to our past. We have moments of *choice* and acting on those can change the direction of the rest of our life. A simple example: Phil is not known for his honesty. His view of life is that it is everyone for himself and that, if other people are not sharp enough to work the system, that is their problem. He lies whenever it is convenient and whenever he thinks he can get away with it. One day he gets a call from his sister. Her son has been picked up for shoplifting. The boy's father has remarried and left the area and Phil's sister is desperate. Could Phil please talk to him? Phil's no saint when it comes to shoplifting and lying to get out of trouble. But he does know what it means to have a police record and he always liked his nephew. He'd much rather go on the skiing trip he had planned this weekend and he could avoid his sister's request easily enough. He's an expert at phony excuses. But after reflection (a rarity for Phil) he makes a decision to talk to his nephew. In one of the most honest conversations of his life Phil tells his nephew about his own self-destructive experiences and offers honestly to be available when or if his nephew needs him.

Now, prior to this, Phil's character had already been shaped in a certain direction. As the Hindus might say, Phil's upbringing and earlier choices in life were like waves that have built up sand bars in the lake of his mind. Soon the sand bars themselves focus and direct the waves; his future thoughts and actions are channeled by habits built up earlier in his lifetime. In Phil's case the habit of deceit played a big role in channeling his actions. But it *is* possible to go against engrained habits, to willfully change one's character. Such a change can be incredibly difficult; to follow the Hindu metaphor again, moving that packed sand in the lake of your mind can be the most exhausting work you ever do. Phil's decision may be the beginning of such a character change. Then again it may be a wave that slides by the sand bar of deceit and will never be heard of again. Character consists of deeply engrained habits but those habits can be changed bit-by-bit through incremental choices we make on a daily basis.

Harmful habits can come in different forms. Some habits prevent individuals from dealing productively with the world around them. For example, a habit of short-term pleasure seeking, the constant desire for immediate gratification, can prevent a person from making intelligent decisions. Sarah always got her way as a child; now her credit card debt piles up in order to keep her life-style intact. Other habits may be harmful to the actual physical or mental well-being of the person. Overeating is a classic example. Still other habits become powerful addictions. Besides the obvious example of hard drugs like heroine or crack, more common addictions like smoking and alcohol certainly would count here. Negative habits often have all three effects. Alcohol addiction can prevent a man from being a good father, it might be killing him, and it is an addiction over which he senses no control.

What does courage have to do with all this? Let's use addiction as the example of a powerful negative habit that is extremely difficult to break. First, the future without the habit is unknown. A common fact about powerful negative habits is that they often occupy a large portion of a person's life. A significant amount of time, energy and money may go into them, whether it be smoking, alcohol, gambling or an addiction to the Internet. One reason the addicted person is afraid is that the future without the habit is unknown or, if known, it is frightening. Joe goes to the casino as often as he can. He loves the thrill of gambling and, besides, he does not then have to face the fact that his relationship with his wife has deteriorated significantly. Dealing honestly with his gambling habit and his marital problem might mean separation, loneliness, and unknown future relationships, all things he does not want to deal with. Even if Joe knows his wife would be willing to discuss his gambling, he may not want to face the anger, the sorrow, the anguish of an encounter. Much easier to feed the gambling habit. Psychological courage in this case involves facing a future without the addiction and confronting some painful times in his marriage. However, courage also might result in Joe's genuine growth as a person—a deeper self-understanding and a richer, warmer relationship with his spouse. Getting there is a risk—no guarantees about a positive result. But, without courage, Joe will never find out.

Besides facing an unknown future, a second reason the addicted person might need courage is that breaking the habit itself could actually be very painful. This is clearly true in physiologically based addictions. Breaking the smoking habit often involves courage both because the future without a cigarette is anxiety-producing but also because the actual withdrawal can be painful. In some addictions the physical pain of withdrawal may clearly dominate and, since the addicted person is aware of that pain, a willingness to deal with it takes real courage.

A third reason some destructive habits are hard to break is self-image. This is especially true for habits hidden from the general public. Alcoholism is a prime example. Each of us likes to present a positive image to the world and admitting a personal failure is often a fearful prospect. Much more will be said about self-image in the course of the book, but at this point I want to emphasize the simple courage it takes to look at other people and admit that "I made a mistake" or "I have failed" in some way. This act deserves far more recognition as an act of courage. Covering up our mistakes to look good is cowardice. How difficult this facet of psychological courage is depends a good deal on how society views the act in question and how deeply we have falsified our image to people around us. It is especially difficult if a person has projected a radically different image from her actual behavior. A woman may cultivate her image as a loving mother and in so doing keeps her alcoholism a secret in every way she can. She simply cannot reveal her secret life. This type of scenario is not unusual—none of us completely matches the image we like to project to the world. The greater the gap between the image and reality, the greater the courage it takes to admit the truth.

We may need psychological courage to face an unknown future or to face the physical pain of changing a bad habit. But perhaps the most profound challenge to courage is to admit that what we have projected as our self is a fraud. Our fear of admitting this is based on the threat of psychological annihilation, a total loss of self brought on by the destruction of our self-image. The courage to admit weakness is the beginning of real strength but we are afraid to take that chance. We are afraid there would be no "self" left at all without the rationalizations and the false image we have set up. How and why we protect our self-image at all costs and refuse to admit mistakes is so central a part of our everyday life that it is important to explore the reasons in more detail.

COURAGE AND SELF-JUSTIFICATION

During the court-martial of Lieutenant William Calley for his role in the slaughter of innocent civilians at My Lai, his psychiatrist reported that the lieutenant came to regard the Vietnamese people as less than human. . . . Social psychologists have learned that people do not perform acts of cruelty and come out unscathed. I do not know for sure how Lieutenant Calley (and thousands of others) came to regard the Vietnamese as subhuman, but it seems reasonable to assume that, when we are engaged in a war in which, through our actions, a great number of innocent people are being killed, we might try to derogate the victims in order to justify our complicity in the outcome. We might poke fun at them, refer to them as "gooks," dehumanize them; but, once we have succeeded in doing that, watch out—because it becomes easier to hurt and kill "subhumans" than to hurt and kill fellow human beings.

Elliot Aronson, *The Social Animal*, 7th edition, 221

People cover up mistakes and dodge unpleasant truths in several ways. Let's review a map, so to speak, of psychological cowardice. Imagine buying a new car and investing a good deal of your savings to do so. Just your luck, you find out that three months ago *Consumer Reports* published a detailed and careful study of your car and judged it the worst model of the year in terms of performance and safety. Moreover, you soon read in the paper that another independent evaluation came to the same conclusion. You did not do your homework. How will you handle that negative evidence? You are not usually a dishonest person. Will you say, "Well, I goofed. I may have made a poor investment. I'll just have to live with it." Or might you say something like "Those independent evaluators really aren't so independent, you know. They often have ties to companies they promote." Or "Yeah, there have been some problems with that model but mine is different." This tendency to justify actions in which we have a great deal invested has been spelled out in a powerful way in social psychology by what is called "cognitive dissonance theory."[1] In this section I want to specify the courage it takes to deal with dissonance in an honest way.

Simply put, cognitive dissonance theory says that when we have two "cognitions" that clash with each other (dissonance) the state of tension produced demands some resolution. Generally the more time, energy or money you have invested in the situation, the greater the tension. There is little cognitive dissonance between two conflicting mathematical ideas you happen to have (unless of course you're a mathematician). But enormous dissonance would exist if you thought your spouse was a trustworthy person and you now have evidence of infidelity. Dissonance is a deeply-embedded aspect of human life because thoughts and actions on which we base our lives are frequently challenged by contradictory evidence.

How do people deal with dissonance? One way is to face the truth and act appropriately. But that may be the exception because, as noted above, we do not want to admit mistakes. Two other ways that avoid dissonance without facing reality are 1) *downplay* the disturbing cognition or 2) *add* cognitions in order to weaken the disturbing one.[2] Imagine dissonance caused by smoking or adultery. Downplaying the disturbing cognition would mean saying things to yourself like "The evidence about smoking is really mixed" or "One fling is not the same as being unfaithful." If this strategy is successful then the tension is reduced between the cognitions "I am a rational person" and "I smoke" or between "I love my spouse" and "I just had sex with another person." The importance of the cognition about smoking or sex is lowered, thus allowing both cognitions to co-exist in the mind. This can also be done by relabeling the disturbing cognition, which is simply a shorthand way of downgrading it. So "heavy smoker" becomes "moderate smoker" and "adulterer" becomes "man going through mid-life crisis."

The strategy of adding new cognitions might take the form of "Yes, smoking is dangerous but I like to live on the edge" or "Reducing my anxiety by smoking is well worth the danger." In the case of the affair it might be "Yes, I was unfaithful but variety is critical to keeping a long-term relationship going" or "Sex with someone else will improve the sex life in our marriage." These justifications are not direct attacks on the evidence or the worth of the dissonant ideas. Instead, they act like a "bridge" between the two cognitions and reduce dissonance by accepting both but trying to weld them together. "I am rational and I am doing a dangerous thing in smoking but reducing my anxiety is *worth* it." This addition ties the first two cognitions together and reduces dissonance.

Habits may or may not be involved in the dissonance problem. But one habit is always important and that is how we have learned to deal with dissonance. Children can learn early on that getting out of a problem by ignoring evidence or by adding false or exaggerated ideas can make them feel better. A child's dissonance between "My parents think I am a good person" and "I just kicked the neighbor's dog" can be justified by "The dog deserved it because . . ." (added cognition) or "It wasn't really a 'kick.'" (downplay disturbing cognition). You hear this sort of excuse constantly from children. Good parenting will help children avoid this tendency and help reinforce dealing with dissonance honestly. Learning to face the truth courageously is critical for development of a child's full potential; otherwise, self-justification and distorting reality to cover up dissonance can easily become a habit. Children grow up thinking that dodging evidence or making up excuses is how to deal with difficult or tension-producing situations in life. Bluntly put, this behavior as a child is a blueprint for psychological cowardice as an adult.

Dealing with cognitive dissonance is thus a deeply personal issue involving courage. But justifying our thoughts and actions irrationally can also have devastating effects on those around us. By downplaying evidence or adding false or exaggerated cognitions, our range of choices becomes focused not by reality but by the set of ideas needed to avoid the issue. For example, if an act of spousal abuse creates significant dissonance in the abuser, the abuser may justify it by claiming the spouse deserved it or the act wasn't really that bad. Then, when similar situations arise in the future, it will be easier to justify further abuse because the groundwork has already been laid. It's already been established that the spouse deserves it and a range of actions has already been deemed acceptable in the abuser's mind. The same mechanism often functions with acts of prejudice. A habit of avoiding responsibility for the results of our actions becomes acceptable and future acts divorcing the self from responsibility can fit a pattern established earlier. That pattern may well have started with the original need to reduce dissonance.

Dissonance reduction can therefore be a major factor in justifying cruelty toward others. Most people consider themselves to be decent human beings. But imagine you have a harmful thought about someone and enjoy it, or imagine getting a good feeling out of seeing someone else hurt. Both of these are dissonant with "I am a good person." How do we deal with such facts about our inner life? A little psychological courage allows us to face such thoughts and feelings honestly, admit weaknesses in ourselves, and look for genuine reasons why such feelings and thoughts occur. But it is all too easy to slip into self-justification. A classic example of this mentioned by Aronson is the study done after the killing of the students on the Kent State campus during the Vietnam War.[3] People in the community (and elsewhere) believed all sorts of rumors to justify the dissonance between their self-image ("I am a good person who does not believe in killing innocent people") and the fact that they wanted to justify the shooting of the students. The students shot were supposedly covered with lice or they all had syphilis. All the rumors were false but they made people comfortable by reducing dissonance.

Dissonance reduction through distorting our concepts is pervasive and common and so completely irrational that, were it not for the devastating consequences, it would be comical. Consider the following study by psychologists Keith Davis and Edward Jones.[4] They convinced a group of students to volunteer for an experiment and then asked them one by one to watch another student being interviewed. The students doing the observing knew nothing about the character of the student being watched. No matter what they actually thought after watching the interview, they were told by the experimenter to tell the student they saw interviewed that he was shallow, untrustworthy and dull. Amazingly, even though the observing students knew full well that they did not have any prior knowledge of the person being observed, after telling him harmful things about his character based on no evidence whatsoever, a later survey of the observers showed that they *convinced themselves* that the person really was shallow, untrustworthy and dull. After all, the observers were good people and they had to say some pretty terrible things to this person so, obviously, he must have deserved it.

Self-justification also played a role in the famous Milgram experiment in which people were told to shock a learner up to 450 volts for wrong answers.[5] (No shocks were actually received but the "teachers" clearly thought they were.) You are a good person yet you just shocked an innocent man with 100 volts. It must be OK—he didn't say anything. At 150 volts the man cries out. What to do? I've committed myself to this experiment and said I would do what I was told and, besides, it's not my responsibility. It's the scientist in the white coat giving orders. With such dissonance-reducing reasons, over 50% of the participants shocked an innocent man with progressive 15 volt increments up to 450 volts. The "teachers" heard the victim screaming and begging for release and, for the last 100 volts or so, there was total silence in the adjacent room, a clear indication that the "learner" might be unconscious or dead. Yet over 50% went all the way.

In Milgram's book and the film of the experiment you can see psychological courage as well as moral courage in action. At 150 volts, when the person first cries out, many "teachers" hesitate and Milgram's assistant says to go on. Many refused and Milgram's assistant says "You have no choice." Some of the teachers then said, "Yes, I have a choice. I refuse." Some succumbed to further pressure but many held their ground. What is happening here? First, moral courage plays a major role because these people stood up for the protection of an innocent person against the social pressure of the experimenter. But psychological courage permeates this setting also. Each and every one of those participants had to make a choice: either face the results of their actions honestly or accept a dissonance-reducing excuse so they could maintain a positive self-image while continuing to obey the experimenter. To face the facts honestly meant admitting to themselves what exactly they were doing. It meant looking bad in front of the experimenter and taking a blow to their projected self-image. Psychological courage meant finding the strength to face *themselves* without using excuses. Without psychological courage moral courage would not have been a live option.

As you might guess, studies show that people with high self-esteem or a positive self-image experience more dissonance when they behave in a stupid or cruel way. After all, they have a strong, well-established self-image and they just acted like a fool or worse. Conversely, people with a low self-image experience much less dissonance when they act cruelly or stupidly. Again, the reason is not hard to understand. Their actions more closely match their self-image. This difference has results in practical behavior. Persons with low self-esteem find it easier to commit cruel or stupid acts whereas people with high self-esteem resist more. Just how important this factor is has been shown in an experiment by Aronson and Mettee, an experiment which in itself poses some ethical problems.[6] They predicted that even a temporary blow to a person's self-esteem would make it easier for the person to do an unlawful or unethical act. They had a group of students take a personality test. Randomly, one third were told the results showed they were mature, deep and interesting people. Another third were told it showed they lacked maturity, were shallow and needed to live more interesting lives. The final third was told nothing. Then the whole group was put in an experiment by another psychologist which they thought was totally unrelated to the personality test. It was a card game involving betting and money in which cheating was easy and thought to be undetectable and cheating could clearly lead to winning. The results followed exactly from what they were told on the personality test. Those who received information that lowered their self-esteem cheated much more than the others. Those who got the positive information cheated least and the group told nothing fell exactly between.

Courage thus seems "easier" for people who have high self-esteem and high self-confidence. This goes for courage of all types. But keep in mind two provisos here. High self-esteem and high self-confidence can be a facade, especially in our capitalist system in which sales are rarely made by people who don't look confident. Looking confident may have little to do with how you really feel about yourself. Second, overconfidence can be a significant problem. A danger of any virtue is that, once established, it is taken as a given. So, for example, the genuine and caring physician may be so confident in her character that she begins to ignore her mistakes. After all, she *is* genuine and caring. Likewise, the habit of facing dissonance honestly may, in an odd way, become such a given that laziness sneaks in the back door. Courage is never easy and, when it appears to be so, we may be most in danger of losing it.

Given these provisos, the courage to face our own weaknesses and faults is genuinely enhanced if we are confident in our own strength of character. This too has important implications for child-rearing. "Self-esteem" as the result of unconditional love has its role for a young child but eventually it should have something to do with what a child *does*. Very few children will be great athletes or intellectual stars, but all children will face the challenge of knowing themselves and acting with (or without) integrity. If a child can be encouraged and supported to face his or her own weaknesses and to deal with them honestly, the child can begin a path to high self-esteem that is deserved, regardless of whether our economic and social system recognizes great external achievements. Such external achievements definitely deserve recognition but many who do achieve external success have little courage when it comes to facing themselves, their weaknesses, and their fears. Regardless of whatever else parents may help their child achieve, to guide a child to a life of integrity is surely the greatest moral legacy parents can leave behind them.

COURAGE AND SELF-DECEPTION

A ship owner was about to send to sea an immigrant ship. He knew that she was old, and not over well built at the first; that she had seen many seas and climes, and often had needed repairs. Doubts had been suggested to him that possibly she was not seaworthy. These doubts preyed upon his mind, and made him unhappy; he thought this should put him to great expense. Before the ship sailed, however, he succeeded in overcoming these melancholy reflections. He said to himself that she had gone safely through so many voyages and weathered so many storms that it was idle to suppose she would not come safely home from this trip also. He would put his trust in Providence, which could hardly fail to protect all these unhappy families that were leaving their fatherland to seek for better times elsewhere. He would dismiss from his mind all ungenerous suspicions about the honesty of builders and contractors. In such ways he acquired a sincere and comfortable conviction that his vessel was thoroughly safe and seaworthy; he watched her depart with a light heart, and benevolent wishes for the success of the exiles in their strange new home that was to be; and he got his insurance money when she went down in mid-ocean and told no tales.

W.K. Clifford cited in Bela Szabados, "The Self, Its Passions, and Self-Deception" in *Self-Deception and Self-Understanding*, edited by Mike W. Martin, 156.

Self-justification can be seen as one form of a larger human phenomenon — self-deception. If we reduce dissonance by irrational means, the reason we do it is because we *know* a conflict exists. This knowledge may or may not be conscious but our emotional state of tension gives away the fact that we are aware of the dissonance. How often do people in full awareness reduce dissonance by irrational means? For example, going back to the smoking case, how common is it for people to say: "Yes, I smoke and know about the evidence showing how dangerous it is and I know I am a rational person. I will downgrade the evidence knowing full well that my view is an exaggerated one whose only purpose is to allow me to continue smoking." The answer to the previous question is: Never. Why? Because if you knew that your downgrading of the evidence was designed only to let you keep smoking, the whole point of doing it would be lost and dissonance would not be reduced. In order to be successful in irrationally reducing dissonance you have to some degree convince yourself that your distortion of the evidence or your added cognition ("doctors smoke; it must be OK") is true. Yet the rational you, the you who goes through life trying to make the best and most rational decisions, knows that it is not true. You know at some level that you are reducing dissonance simply to maintain the smoking habit. This co-existence of truth and lying to yourself is the heart is what is called self-deception.

The Levels of Self-Deception

In the last fifty years philosophers have spent quite some time discussing self-deception. I want to pick out certain areas that are directly relevant to psychological courage. In an excellent analysis of this issue the philosopher Mike Martin has distinguished five tactics of self-deception.[7] They also can be viewed as levels or degrees of self-deception, though in fact they often permeate each other. Utilizing these divisions is helpful for looking at how each and everyone of us can deceive ourselves in daily life and how courage can help us face the truth.

The tactic of "willful ignorance" can be viewed as the lowest level of self-deception. Willful ignorance is keeping ourselves unaware of some information which we know would disturb us. Whether we do this or not again comes back to preserving a certain safe self-identity. If you think there might be a problem with your car and you don't have a lot of spare money at the moment, there's a good chance you will ignore the problem, perhaps for a long time. But, despite the financial and time problems involved in fixing it, it is unlikely that you would actually deceive yourself about it. A somewhat dated term in psychology still fits here. You "suppress" the information but the information is still available to you. You might well admit that you are lax about looking into it but you can accept the truth.

Now the situation is quite different, for example, if you have a clue that your partner is cheating on you. After all, you have a great deal of your self invested in the person. You have been together socially many times and your self-image is tied, at least to some degree, to that relationship. You have opened yourself emotionally and trusted the person. Because of the threat to psychological stability, when you first get a hint of possible negative evidence, you avoid all possible situations where that knowledge might appear. A person can become quite good at this. This is "willful ignorance."

This stage in self-deception is important because at this level you still have not developed a series of full-blown lies or cover-ups. It is at this stage that psychological courage early on can prevent a much greater problem later. A person needs to be emotionally aware when he or she begins to avoid information. Ask yourself: Why am I doing this? Am I trying to hide something? What emotions or what part of my self-image am I trying to protect? There is a particular emotion—a variation of fear—that fleetingly announces to you that you *need* to keep yourself ignorant. Courage involves being aware of that feeling, asking yourself some honest questions, and ultimately facing reality.

The second tactic of self-deception is called "systematic ignoring." Initially this might look like the previous one but there is one important difference. Here the evidence is apparent; you are not keeping yourself separate from ever knowing the information. It's all there but you refuse to acknowledge it. We use at least two techniques to keep ourselves from admitting such truths. The first has been called "blocking," perhaps in therapeutic terms, "repression." Quite simply we keep the information out of our conscious awareness. As Martin notes, part of this is preventing the information from becoming the focus of attention.[8] It's OK at the margins of our thought because there it can be ignored. But it must at all costs be prevented from becoming the central focus of attention. In most cases it is simply easier to block it altogether. But, in certain situations or certain conversations, the information may be forced on us and then our best maneuver is to try to keep it in the margins. Imagine Brian is deceiving himself about his success in his career. A person who chooses any career does not choose failure; he invests himself in it, often a great deal of himself. But not everyone is successful and admitting that can be one of the most difficult moments in a person's life. Some willful ignorance by Brian clearly could help avoid the issue. But if the job evaluations or the results of interaction with others clearly make the point, more drastic measures would have to be taken. Evidence must be systematically ignored and blocking it would be a major way to do this. If it did come up, keeping the evidence of failure at the margins of thought would allow Brian to focus attention on harmless areas and keep the facade of success alive.

A second related technique for systematically ignoring truth is through distraction. Brian has learned that, when he begins to think about his lack of success in his profession, he can dodge the problematic areas by distracting himself with other ideas — perhaps meaningless statistics or personal relationships developed in his job or maybe his planned vacation. In conversations with others he becomes a master at distracting the conversation to other topics. Other people may think of him as a superb conversationalist but part of the reason is that he has become an expert at switching topics in an interesting way because there are some places he does not want to go. Keep in mind that "distraction" in this sense does not mean avoiding issues for rational reasons. After all, personal lives are not the property of the general public and distracting or changing topics may well be justified in many cases. (The media love to confuse genuine privacy with the "need" to hide something.) In discussing self-deception the term means avoiding areas because you do not *want* to face them. It is a way to avoid being honest with yourself.

Psychological courage is a significantly more difficult virtue here. The initial moment of fear, which can lead a person to remain ignorant, has become a terror that must be covered up. The root of the terror is the fear of psychological annihilation. Brian feels that admitting the truth would be so devastating that his self could not survive. Unlike the issues discussed in later chapters, self-deception is not something people usually consider as a subject for therapy or counseling. Perhaps the biggest help in overcoming this level of self-deception is friendship. I will discuss the importance of friendship in some length in the last chapter but at this point the key is that a close friend is not threatening. A close friend is a type of counselor for self-honesty — someone who, because you trust her, can actually guide you into territory which would otherwise terrify you. Ultimately, you must decide to go there yourself and to be strong enough to avoid blocking or distraction. But this is a journey made much more bearable by someone else being with you.

The third tactic of self-deception is "emotional detachment." This is not so much a different level as it is an effect that accompanies other degrees of self-deception. The noticeable characteristic here is an emotional coolness or aloofness when ideas are brought up which a person wants to hide from herself. If a parent is deceiving herself about her child in some way, perhaps about his behavior as an adolescent, when that topic rises in consciousness or in conversation with others, she will maintain emotional distance from it. The reason is straightforward. Emotions engage us with the world around us, whether it be love, anger, admiration or any other emotion. An emotional response to evidence about her son's behavior would force the parent to engage in it in a way that would force the issue to consciousness. As long as intellect can be cut off from feelings, we can compartmentalize events or ideas in a way that keeps us safe from any unpleasant implications. Emotions are a form of *recognition*. Anger, sorrow, frustration or love in response to her son's actual behavior makes self-deception much more difficult. The lie's transparency is exposed. So emotional detachment is critical in both remaining deliberately ignorant and in systematically ignoring a truth.

Psychological courage in dealing with this tactic means being willing to engage the truth emotionally. It is possible that this aspect of courage may "precede" in a way the courage to actually face the truth. The hidden truth always has certain emotional connotations. For example, refusing to face her son's behavior may exist because of a feeling of loss or failure on her part. The initial engagement with the idea involves some negative emotion which the mother does not want to feel. Emotional detachment is a way of avoiding that feeling. *Courage can come into play by admitting into our bodily sensations emotions which we are afraid to face.* There is a moment, especially early on in the self-deceptive process, when the person is aware of that negative emotion prior to the intellect blocking and compartmentalizing the information. The moment of courage lies in that moment. If the self-deception has become habitual, then there may be very little leeway for recognizing *any* emotion. But many times self-deception does leave a tiny crack open for the true emotion to appear, however briefly. Avoiding emotional detachment and accepting ownership of that emotion is another variant of psychological courage.

A fourth tactic in self-deception is "self-pretense." This is beyond (in a sense) willful ignorance and systematic ignoring because at this stage the person accepts the evidence or truth of the situation but covers up the implication with excuses and false justifications. In the above example, yes, the son has stolen many times and hurt some innocent people. But the police have always had it in for him and that group he hangs around with led him astray. He is not responsible for his actions because his father was too strict and he is just rebelling. Now, whether or not there is any truth in these claims is irrelevant because the purpose of their expression is to prevent what the son is doing from coming to full consciousness in the mother. Why? Again, for the two reasons discussed above. If the mother accepts fully what the son is doing, her fear is that the image of herself she has maintained will be annihilated. It is likely she has publicly expressed these excuses and publicly attempted to maintain the false image of her son. Admission at this point involves both an admission of personal and social failure. Moreover, the emotions that would have to be faced would be traumatic. Any parent can relate to what she would feel. At this point in the process courage is catching yourself *before* expressing the excuse and then choosing to live without excuses. Since it is likely that self-pretense is often a follow up to willful ignorance and systematic ignoring, courage becomes more difficult because a pattern has been laid down.

Self-pretense blends into the deepest stage of self-deception, a level which I consider one of the most dangerous mental conditions in the world in terms of harming innocent people. Martin calls this stage "rationalization" which confuses it somewhat with other tactics in self-deception.[9] Perhaps a better term for it would simply be "intellectual delusion." At this level the person not only puts forth excuses and false justifications but actually comes to believe them. Then, as the phrase says, anything goes.

First, however, an important proviso. Keep in mind that we are talking about *self*-deception. Frequently people lie or make excuses because of external threats—loss of a job, for example. In such cases the degree of self-deception is often minimal. Frank may know full well that he is not putting in the time he should on those engineering designs. But in order to keep his job he lies about it. This is dishonesty but it probably is not self-deception. For the straightforward liar, telling the truth and refusing to make excuses under conditions such as Frank's would fall more under moral courage. In such cases it's unlikely (but possible) that Frank would actually come to believe what he says because he knows full well why he is lying—to save his job. The relationship between lying to others and lying to yourself can have many forms. Lying to others can be completely separate from lying to yourself, i.e., the person would simply be a "liar". Lying to others can be partially tied into lying to yourself, e.g., the hypocrite who puts out a false front to people and partially believes it himself. Hypocrisy is closely tied to self-pretense with the addition that the hypocrite usually advertises in some way a false positive image. Most hypocrites, however, are not totally delusional about the truth. At the delusional level lying to others is completely linked to self-deception.

It's at this last level that self-deception is most dangerous. National political leader John Smith has had to do some lying to get into office and, once there, has had to make some deals to stay there, deals that have hurt several innocent people. At first John simply avoided thinking about what happened. After all, he had won and times were good. He couldn't afford the emotional involvement and, politically, he had to be "above" that anyway. Then, after several constituents and the press started to bring the issue to awareness, John began making excuses and justifications. Wasn't it true, after all, that, while some people were hurt, what he did was good for the nation overall? And what choice did he really have? John only half-heartedly believed these claims; he knew what he did was a self-serving political maneuver but the justifications seemed to be selling OK to the public. And they did keep him in office with a positive image. Then a strange thing began to happen. John began to believe his own excuses and justifications. What served John's interests really *was* good for the country and he really *had* no other choice. Now, having lost a reality check completely, John realized that tapping the phones of his enemies was a great idea for the security of the nation and that nothing kept order like having troops use maximum force against those protesters. John's justifications were all straightforward. Other people had the odd feeling that John was lying somehow, that all this was a front but, when they looked at John, he seemed sincere. People can spot hypocrites; John didn't seem like a hypocrite. He *believed* what he said.

This scenario I would argue has been played out time after time in history by political and religious leaders who have come to believe their own justifications. It is incredibly dangerous because the individual in power can then justify anything because he has become completely habitualized to deceiving himself. Surely God wants me to ask for generous donations and my investment of that money in a palatial home reinforces the glory of God. Surely that other ethnic group is truly evil and what choice does one have with true evil except to obliterate all of it? Humans have been known as "rational animals" but, given history, perhaps we should be known as the "self-deceptive animals." How many humans can actually do what we have done to each other and be fully aware of it intellectually and emotionally? A few with antisocial personality disorder already have the interpersonal emotions blunted but I would argue that the vast majority of the cruelty done to others is performed by people who have progressed by degrees to a deep level of self-deception.[10] At such a level psychological courage is rarely an issue because such courage requires a goal defined by truth and, without an internal reality check, no image of truth exists to counter the lie. Delusional people can actually include within their scheme at times a false kind of courage—a kind of "courage" to do the destructive act. (It took "courageous leadership" to send the militia into that village.) This is yet another front for self-deception. Genuine psychological courage is extremely relevant in less profound stages of self-deception. Those fleeting moments of truth and honest emotions are doors through which we can choose to enter. If society can come to praise such courage and reinforce it, perhaps we will have less cases of abuse of power by deeply self-deceived individuals.

The Morality of Self-Deception

I want to close this section by asking a fundamental question about self-deception. Is it ever good? Put another way, are there times when we ought to avoid the truth, times in which psychological courage about facing the truth would not be a benefit? Philosophers have given several possible reasons why self-deception might be beneficial. I want to summarize some of these claims and clarify how psychological courage would still be a factor.

The examples designed to show self-deception in a positive light are ones in which a "greater good" is produced by deceiving yourself. This type of argument is an example of utilitarianism, a view in ethics that says each situation should be judged by the number and breadth of good consequences. The utilitarian claim is that situations exist in which self-deception would produce more good than harm. For example, it has been argued that in some marriages deceiving yourself about your spouse's infidelity may be better overall for the stability of the marriage and the children.[11] Utilitarianism argues that life is neither fair nor reasonable and self-honesty in certain marriages might have more destructive consequences than willful ignorance or systematic ignoring of the truth. Another example given is a life-long friendship in which one of the friends has been embezzling small amounts from a joint business.[12] The argument goes that, given the rarity and value of a long-term friendship, willful ignorance of the embezzling might be the best way to go.

Such cases are ones where lack of courage in facing the truth is an apparent virtue. But in these examples other options are considered worse than self-deception without evidence to support that claim. Often self-deception is simply easier. In the friendship example, on the surface it seems obvious that goods built up over a lifetime are not sacrificed easily and self-deception over one element (the friend's siphoning off business funds) is worth it. But what is not discussed is the effect of self-deception itself on the friendship and the business. With self-deception a major qualitative difference enters the friendship. The blocking which occurs in self-deception, especially over something as important as the shared business, cannot but affect the emotional tone between the friends. What was before an open, genuine (perhaps naive) relationship is now one in which certain areas of conversation and thought are systematically blocked. If friendship means anything, it means openness and trust. The friendship is qualitatively changed in a destructive way by the self-deception. Moreover, it is not at all clear that maintaining a business with a partner who is embezzling is a good idea. In this case courage in facing this issue might lead to the loss of the friendship and the business but it might also deepen the friendship and improve the business. It's a risk but courage is always a risk. Very often avoiding courage because of "good reasons" is a cover for fear.

The same point would hold for the marriage example. Is deceiving yourself worth it for the sake of the children? Again the utilitarians ignore what might be called the "radiating effect" of self-deception. What would self-deception about your spouse's affair do to other parts of the relationship? Conversation? Your own shared sex life? The sharing of pains and joys in life? This is not some small isolated event. If any of these other areas in the marriage happened to touch on the truth, then they would have to papered over with a false front or else avoided. Self-deceivers cannot let their guard down or the deception fails; they have to invent a "cover story" to keep themselves and others involved in the deception. Besides, children are not stupid. They often, perhaps most of the time, recognize emotional dissonance easier than adults. Maintaining self-deception for a positive good in this case is most likely a fantasy. Psychological courage would be enormously difficult. You might lose the marriage and the children. Or, perhaps, you might regain a marriage and what a family is really about.

A better example to support avoidance of the truth has to do with what is commonly called "denial." Traumatic news cannot be absorbed quickly and, utilitarians argue, for some people it cannot be absorbed at all. A quite common example of denial is being told of a terminal illness. An example given by the philosopher Amelie Rorty is of a doctor who is involved in a critical research project who discovers he is terminally ill.[13] Rorty claims that deceiving himself about the illness may be completely justified so that he can continue with a positive attitude on the project he loves. Rorty's example is really a variation on a common theme in psychology. Denial is valuable in cases such as terminal illness because it allows a person time to adjust and complete projects which may require full attention.

But denial of the truth is a temporary good at best. Certainly it takes time for us to absorb traumatic news and nothing is more difficult to accept than one's own death. But denial is an important "stage." Counselors attempt to help patients through this stage. Put another way, counselors (or close friends again) try to help the person be courageous. People not only have to deal with closure in external events but they should be able, if at all physically possible, to close the book on their personal relationships and deepest inner thoughts and feelings. You cannot close the book if you refuse to recognize that it will end. In Rorty's example, perhaps the personality of the physician requires denial but I have more faith in the ability of people to face and deal with tragedies, even people with tendencies toward melancholy as Rorty says about this doctor. Her case is certainly possible but in acknowledging self-deception as good we are acquiescing in it and, in dealing with this physician, we would have to support it in conversation. This pattern of paternalism and humoring someone because he cannot face the truth is in many ways a thoroughly disrespectful way of treating an adult in his last days of life. Perhaps other options are available. Lack of considered options is a problem for many utilitarian justifications of self-deception.

I want to present three more examples, one a defense of self-deception because the event is trivial, another because the event is monstrous, and a third based on a society that one cannot escape. Robert Audi gives what he specifically considers a trivial or minor example of self-deception.[14] A teacher who loves her students and wants them to like her convinces herself that one student's hostile behavior in one of her courses is not due to actual hostility toward her but due to the student's own insecurity. This is a more complex case than it appears since such hostility by students *is* at times related to insecurity. But let's take it at face value. This seems to be a harmless case of self-deception. It does not involve traumatic or life-threatening events and seems limited to one student this teacher has in class. But even simple examples like this ignore the radiating effect of self-deception. It is unlikely that only one student in one course will display hostility or disdain for any given teacher. Any experienced teacher will run into students who simply do not like one's style, personality, organization of material, the class, and so on. Moreover, and probably more important, outside of the classroom individuals frequently run into situations in which they very much want approval but are not given it. How is a person going to respond to such situations? The key here is that the *motivation* in this case, the need to be liked, is not context-specific. The teacher's need to be liked is so intense that she deceives herself about the apparent facts of the student's behavior. This is a character trait that will carry over into several possible situations. The most likely scenario for the teacher is that this case is not a special circumstance but an example of a pattern, a habit. So psychological courage in even small matters—one student and why he or she dislikes you—can begin to break a habit and start a positive cycle for facing reality more effectively.

People can deceive themselves about their feelings ("I am not angry"), about their skills ("I cannot do this job" or "I can fix anything"), about truth in nature ("all that evidence about the dinosaurs and the age of the earth is a hoax"), about a truth in their lives ("I am not an alcoholic") or about truth in society ("That other ethnic group deserves what it gets"). Courage (along with much needed support) can defeat all of these. But the last two provide certain types of examples that imply psychological cowardice may be the best path at times. Consider Beth who was severely abused as a child and is now an adult. As an adult Beth's life is very difficult but there are moments of genuine liberation through her artwork and dance classes. Beth deceives herself a great deal about what happened to her as a child. A close friend who knows Beth's past and her current self-deception tries to work with Beth to help her understand what she is blocking. As she does so, it becomes apparent that, when Beth starts to trace a path of self-honesty, her world begins to disintegrate. The trauma of the childhood abuse is so profound and so deeply engrained in her psyche that it genuinely appears that personality disintegration may result from delving into it. Courage on Beth's part is not an issue if there is no self left to act and the level of support needed to establish that renewed identity may be beyond the capability of not just friends but psychiatry in its current state. In such cases is it not better for Beth to have a life of self-deception that includes some moments of liberation rather than a very good likelihood of no life at all? This book is about the enormous value of psychological courage but, if the self truly is so fragile that to reach the choice-point of being courageous is itself impossible, then perhaps self-deception may be the only way to go on. My argument earlier is that a great deal of the defense of self-deception is not based on the evidence but on the fact that it is easier. But there are certainly cases where the evidence itself points to a different path.

One final example of a different sort but which I also find powerful and persuasive. Imagine being born and raised in Stalinist Russia. In the back of your mind you have a hint of what human freedom is but expression of that freedom is deadly. Simple deception is not enough to trick an astute and trained secret police force. Moreover, you never know who might report on you, so you can never afford "leakage" of your true views. You also cannot get out of the society. In this situation it may be critical that you convince yourself of the truth of the propaganda given you. Then you can tell your potential threat with a straight face that you support the fabric of lies. And, even more advantageous, you can use self-deception as a way to weasel your way into a position in which the threat is minimal and in which you would have maximum chance at food and shelter and, possibly, a good mate.

The point here is that social conditions may be so overwhelming that self-deception may be the only way to survive. Some other examples given in this regard are much weaker, e.g., convincing yourself that the product you are selling is worth something when actually you know it is not—all for the sake of surviving in this society. Clearly there are other options in this case, difficult as they may be. But that is not the situation in a blanket totalitarian society. Other values such as family, friends, life itself, might well be impossible if you did not convince yourself that government lies were truth (and that truth was a lie). Of course some of our greatest heroes on behalf of truth have combined psychological courage (accepting truth without self-deception) with the physical courage of facing death, and many have died because of that. And moral courage is a critical issue also because going along with the state almost always means implicitly cooperating in injustice and harm to other innocent people. But it is not clear how wide we should throw the net of courage here. Most if not all readers of this book are not, nor hopefully ever will be, in the situation of choosing death versus self-honesty. But many humans have been forced to make this choice. And the question of whether physical annihilation (along with, possibly, family and friends) by an efficient police state is worth personal self-honesty is not one resolved easily by moral arguments. As Socrates said in the *Crito*. "It is better to live well (meaning ethically) than just to live." But "just living" may include some other profound goods not easily overlooked. So I leave this topic with this question for you the reader: When, really, is self-deception justified?

COMPASSION AND FORGIVENESS

Last year we had a wonderful retreat with Vietnam veterans in America. It was a difficult retreat, because many of us could not get free of our pain. One gentleman told me that in Vietnam, he lost four hundred seventeen people in one battle alone, in one day. Four hundred seventeen men died in one battle, and he has had to live with that for more than fifteen years. . . . One soldier told me that this retreat was the first time in fifteen years that he felt safe in a group of people. For fifteen years, he could not swallow solid food easily. He could only drink some fruit juice and eat some fruit. He was completely shut off and could not communicate. But after three or four days of practice, he began to open up and talk to people. You have to offer a lot of loving kindness in order to help such a person touch things again.

Thich Nhat Hanh (Vietnamese Buddhist monk); *Peace is Every Step*, 102

The example of surviving in a totalitarian society points to the importance of compassion and forgiveness as a balance for courage. We need to be aware of these other virtues for several reasons. First, it is remarkably easy to tell *other* people when they should be courageous—physical, moral or psychological. But the very point of what makes courage a virtue is the risk involved in facing fear for a greater good; the greater the risk the greater the courage.

It is categorically impossible for another individual to experience fully the fear that another person faces for her life or her sanity. We may have had similar experiences but nothing, nothing at all, is like the living moment of choice in the face of danger. So anyone talking about courage or counseling courage *has* to cultivate compassion and empathy for what such situations are like. Otherwise, our counseling is mere pedantry and our words are hollow.

In the same way forgiveness is essential. Everyone of us has failed at times to be courageous. Physical courage demands a set of external conditions which many people may not experience. But situations of moral courage and psychological courage are common. In situations of moral courage how many of us have failed to stand up for what was right? How often has peer pressure or self-image kept us from speaking out when we know we should have? In situations of psychological courage how often do we cover up dissonant ideas and preserve our self-image by giving ourselves phony excuses or downplaying evidence we don't like? How often do we deceive ourselves about our motives or the results of our actions? Since we all fail, we had better not stand too tall when judging others. Forgiveness is a recognition that we are all fragile humans.

But it is also quite possible to use forgiveness as a front for cowardice. If we know others will forgive us or if we forgive ourselves easily, that in itself can become a handy self-deceptive excuse for not taking responsibility for our actions or dealing with fears that need to be dealt with. As Aristotle saw, the key here is balance. Everyone fails and accepting our common fragility is an important part of understanding and accepting who we are. On the other hand, courage and cowardice are real choices, often with profound results, and equally important to our humanity is accepting responsibility for our choices. Somewhere in there is a balance, a mean, and as noted in previous examples, the mean will depend on the person's *history*, the *external conditions* and the *degree of risk*. A person who uses forgiveness as a front for continued failure to make tough decisions does not deserve more forgiveness. He needs to be held responsible for his actions. On the other hand, the person who normally is responsible but fails may well deserve forgiveness. The balance between forgiveness and negative moral judgment is a matter of knowledge and sensitivity and awareness of the conditions which surround the person.

Alcoholism is an example in which forgiveness can be correctly or incorrectly applied. Forgiveness here by either the alcoholic himself or by another individual such as a spouse can be a front for facilitating the habit. Case after case of alcoholism has been facilitated by a wife who continually "forgives" her husband (or vice-versa). Frequently this is a form of denial and self-deception.[15] By using willful ignorance or systematic ignoring, a spouse can remain deliberately blind to what is going on. Or perhaps she uses forgiveness as a front to help justify to herself some exaggeration or half-truth—the effect on the children, the good points of the spouse, the reasons for the drinking. False forgiveness is actually another way of not being courageous.

But genuine forgiveness can also be applied to addictions like alcoholism and AA has done a superb job of doing so. Regardless of how one may feel about AA, in certain ways its procedures are ones that are models for many areas of life. For example, the recognition that "I am an alcoholic," thus taking responsibility for actions, is combined with the recognition that all of the individuals there have also failed. It is a kind of forgiveness with teeth. One of the critical factors in AA is asking the help of others and of a "higher power," however that is conceived. The fact that one is "accepted" by the group and by the higher power after failing in a profound way is a recognition of what forgiveness is—a rejoining into a community (family, friends, humanity) after a failure. The AA example thus shows forgiveness without excuses and the fact that acceptance back into the human community can then be a source of *future* courage. False forgiveness does not lead to future courage; it facilitates cowardice. As with all good counseling and true friendship, in AA someone is there for you on the journey and that makes future acts of psychological courage more bearable. But future decisions are still yours and, even with guidance and help, the courage must come from within you.

AA's model of balancing acceptance after failure with the requirement of future responsibility is one that lies at the heart of human development, from good counseling to raising children. Four-year-old Tricia throws a tantrum because she is afraid to go to bed due to monsters in her room. We of course "forgive" her because she is a child but our response cannot be simply a paternalistic, hollow act. The fear is absolutely real to her. Part of the art of parenting is being able to put oneself in the child's shoes, accept and forgive what is rationally called for, and be on the journey with the child to help her make her own acts of courage. This can be increasingly difficult as a child matures. A teenager who is deceiving himself about popularity, school, or a relationship needs someone on the journey with him in order to be psychologically courageous. Parents, counselors, thoughtful friends—all are candidates. The key, and it is a difficult one, is to forgive and accept when called for, yet help the young person maintain the integrity of personal responsibility.

Two other aspects of courage here are to be able to accept forgiveness and compassion and to be willing to give it. The teenager mentioned above may have great difficulty accepting help from others because that implies a weakness which many teens, with their self insecure to begin with, are loathe to admit. Allowing others to genuinely forgive us and accepting that forgiveness can take great courage. Accepting forgiveness is not a sign of weakness but a path to re-integrating the self—of creating the self again—with the help of others. The same holds for compassion. Admitting you need love, tenderness or caring takes courage because, for males especially, it clashes with the image that society says you are supposed to be like. Fighting off tenderness does not take guts; it's a sign of fear and cowardice about part of yourself. Courage and compassion are complementary virtues, not mutually exclusive ones. It is strange that in practical matters (fixing the plumbing, for example) many more people will admit they are weak and accept help because they know such an admission can improve their lives. But so often humans cannot accept that they are not islands emotionally. They are petrified of relationships that would mean accepting compassion and tenderness from others. Psychological courage is the central virtue for beginning this process.

But courage also is involved in the active willingness to forgive and to be compassionate. The flip side of not being willing to accept forgiveness from others is the fear of genuinely forgiving others. Why is this a fear? A good example occurs in almost all marriages in Western society. Many people marry with an image of their partner that is no longer accurate in one degree or another five or ten years down the road. Perhaps your spouse gives up a high-paying job to go back to school or you simply discover idiosyncrasies you never knew existed. You now have a choice to make, especially if your spouse's actions are unlikely to change. Will you still accept and care about the person? If your spouse has truly failed in some way, are you willing to forgive and work on the relationship? The fear of forgiving a spouse or friend is tied to giving up a previously secure image of what your relationship was and venturing down a new path. The changes in your partner threaten *your* security and forgiving the shortcoming or accepting the changes means not just accepting your spouse's differences but the mutual effect on you. The future may have different emotional overtones and challenges, ones that may expose your own weaknesses. Refusing to forgive, or walking away, is a lot easier. That is why forgiveness of a spouse or friend takes courage. It opens up uncharted waters.

Why does giving tenderness or compassion take courage? Put bluntly, the reason is because we are often scared to death of opening our self and being vulnerable. Many people have been hurt, sometimes badly, by being compassionate and loving. And, even if we have not experienced it personally, we all know of others who have been hurt. So the safe course is to stay locked up inside. But this is no ideal; staying locked up in the self may be necessary for some individuals at certain times but that is a tragedy, not some sort of norm to be taken as a given. Contrary to the "safe" route, the French philosopher Gabriel Marcel argued that "availability," or always being ready to participate in life, is the only path to genuine happiness.[16] As a commentator on Marcel put it, we run around with "bank account" personalities.[17] We are convinced that if we give out too much we will go bankrupt. But the opposite is true. The more deeply we participate, whether with another person or some creative endeavor, the richer life becomes. Yes, we may be hurt and probably will be at times. But what will our response to that pain be? Will it be isolation or the courage to participate? Psychological courage does not mean stupidity. We learn from mistakes so that we can participate and care more wisely. But participate and care we must if life is to be *lived*. That openness to giving compassion, care and love can take tremendous courage.

So how should we balance courage with forgiveness and compassion? The human condition for millions of our species is difficult, often traumatically difficult, from childhood on. Many have limited nutrition, children are being raised as orphans because of AIDS or wars, and plagues continue to threaten societies. Physical as well as psychological pressures can devour people. Perhaps we owe the human race a vast amount of compassion first and foremost; put another way, maybe we should cut each other a great deal of slack when it comes to not being a courageous lot. Simply surviving on some parts of this planet is a full-time job. So what do we do with courage? If we abandon it as an ideal, we have truly lost the game. I would argue that, when details are examined, the small, everyday, unheralded acts of courage—physical, moral, psychological—are central to keeping our species afloat. The mother who risks her own health to gather food for her children, the father who guides his family out of a war zone, the teacher who speaks her conscience against the party line, the addict who for the first time comes to grips with his problem. Millions of small, intensely personal cases of courage are what can turn brute survival into a life that is worth living. Courage, especially psychological courage, lies in the crevices of every human life.

NOTES

1. For a detailed explanation of cognitive dissonance by some of the theory's originators and a classic study of dissonance reduction in action, see Leon Festinger, Henry Riecken, Stanley Schachter, *When Prophecy Fails* (New York: Harper Torchbooks, 1956).

2. See Elliot Aronson, *The Social Animal*, 7th edition (New York: Freeman, 1995), chapter 5.

3. Aronson, *Social Animal*, 218–19.

4. As cited in Aronson, *Social Animal*, 220.

5. Stanley Milgram, *Obedience to Authority* (New York: Harper, 1974).

6. Aronson, *Social Animal*, 226–27.

7. Mike W. Martin, *Self-Deception and Morality* (Lawrence, Kansas: University Press of Kansas, 1986), chapter 2.

8. Martin, *Self-Deception*, 7–8.

9. Martin, *Self-Deception*, 9.

10. Scott Peck argues this point also. His analysis is powerful though he takes self-deception into areas that go well beyond psychology and philosophy. M. Scott Peck, *People of the Lie: The Hope for Healing Human Evil* (New York: Simon and Schuster, 1983).

11. J.W. Meiland, "What Ought We to Believe? or The Ethics of Belief Revisited," *American Philosophical Quarterly* 17, no. 1 (January, 1980): 16. As Martin notes, Tolstoy brilliantly portrays this issue in *Anna Karenina*. Martin, *Self-Deception*, 9–11.

12. Meiland, "Ethics of Belief," 15.

13. Amelie Rorty, "Belief and Self-Deception," *Inquiry* 15 (1972): 401–3.

14. Robert Audi, "Self-Deception and Rationality" in *Self-Deception and Self-Understanding*, ed. Mike W. Martin (Lawrence, Kansas: University Press of Kansas, 1985), 188.

15. See L. Metzger, *From Denial to Recovery: Counseling Problem Drinkers, Alcoholics and their Families* (San Francisco: Jossey-Bass, 1988).

16. Gabriel Marcel, *The Philosophy of Existentialism* (New York: Citadel Press, 1964), 39–43.

17. Sam Keen, *Gabriel Marcel* (Richmond, Virginia: John Knox Press, 1967), 33–34.

Chapter Two

Courage and Anxiety

COURAGE IN THE CAULDRON OF FEAR

A sense of impending danger seemed to descend, spoiling every pleasure, thwarting every ambition. The dread of sudden death, which was at first marked, gradually subsided, giving way more to a feeling of dread—not of dying suddenly—but of doing so under peculiar circumstances or away from home. I became morbidly sensitive about being brought into close contact with any large number of people. Finding myself in the midst of a large gathering would inspire a feeling of terror (which) . . . could be relieved in but one way—by getting away from the spot as soon as possible. Acting on this impulse I have left churches, theatres, even funerals, simply because of an utter inability to control myself to stay. For 10 years I have not been to church, to the theatre, to political gatherings or any form of popular meeting, except where I could remain in the background, with means of egress convenient. Even at my mother's funeral . . . I was utterly unable to bring myself to sit with the other members of the family in the front of the church. Not only has this unfortunate trait deprived me of an immense amount of pleasure and benefit, but it has also been a matter of considerable expense. . . . Time more than I can recall I have gone into restaurants or dining rooms, ordered a meal and left it untouched, impelled by my desire to escape the crowd. . . . I have . . . often . . . walked long distances—perhaps a mile—to avoid crossing some pasture or open square, even when it was a matter of moment to me to have all the time possible . . . .This malady . . . has throttled all ambition, and killed all personal pride, spoiled every pleasure . . . over this the will seems to have no control.

Early case (reported in 1890) of anxiety attacks and agoraphobia cited in C.B. Serignar, M.D., *From Panic to Peace of Mind*, 51–52.

Self-deception and self-justification are common occurrences that force people to make courageous decisions on an almost daily basis. Maintaining a good image in the middle of social interaction constantly pushes us to be less than honest both with others and ourselves. Decisions, even small decisions like promising and then failing to return a phone call, can tempt us to justify our behavior by irrational and cowardly excuses. Moreover, for millions of people negative habits and addictions such as smoking and alcohol can make courage a central virtue in creating a balanced and fulfilling life.

Quite distinct is a category of human behaviors usually listed in psychology texts as anxiety disorders. Clear examples are phobias, obsessions and compulsions. Phobias involve irrational fears of what are in fact harmless or, at worst, cautious situations. Obsessive thoughts and compulsive behaviors can lead to an excess of what is normal, such as cleanliness, or can include acts far outside the norm such as certain irrational rituals.[1] In many habits and addictions pleasure is a big part of the reason we maintain the behavior. But in anxiety disorders the behavior is primarily performed to reduce anxiety and may be done for no other reason. The anxiety is much more the direct cause of the behavior.[2] Fear dominates life.

For example, a person may perform a time-consuming and pointless ritual a hundred times a day and the only reason is to avoid terrifying anxiety. The only "pleasure" involved is negative—avoiding the results of not doing the act. On the other hand, habits like smoking or alcohol have a pleasurable quality about them. Like obsessions and compulsions, fear is still a significant factor to overcome in changing such habits. But with a phobia or compulsion, anxiety literally permeates the individual and becomes if not the sole reason, clearly the overwhelming reason to act. The quality of courage is thus different and the difference lies in the immediate sense of danger. Courage or cowardice are constant companions to the phobic, obsessive, or compulsive person.

I want to focus on one specific example that is quite common—irrational anxiety and anxiety attacks. But, first, if we are going to talk about courage with regard to anxiety, we need to take a look at the word "cowardice" in this context. Does it make sense to use the term "coward" in reference to such psychological problems? The term seems too harsh.

Diagnosing a fear as a psychological problem changes the way we think about it. While we may initially think of someone who refuses an important engagement because he is afraid of heights as being timid or cowardly, when we categorize that fear as a "phobia," such a judgment suddenly appears much more out of place. Why? I suspect one reason is the immediacy of the perceived danger in anxiety disorders and the sense that the person cannot do anything about it. For someone with a fear of heights, nearing any surface edge well above the ground is not perceived as an option. The anxiety is so overwhelming, sometimes even at the thought of it, that any sense of *choice* in confronting the fear or running from it is frequently not present.

This leads to a second reason why the term "coward" applies less easily to anxiety disorders. Destructive habits are associated with a pleasure of some sort—the drug, the cigarette, the drink. Anxiety and pain result from giving up the positive pleasure. With severe anxiety there is no positive state to be achieved except in the odd sort of way that avoiding anxiety is a relief and maintains the status quo. Language such as "he gave up smoking" is premised on the assumption that giving up the pleasure of the habit was worth it to achieve some other goal—health or family life, for example. It would make no sense to say "he gave up his phobia." No positive pleasure exists that must be sacrificed in order to give it up. "Cowardice" as usually used has an element of cravenness in it—taking the short-term good or pleasure in contrast to the higher or nobler good. Anxiety disorders do not present this contrast. With only a negative release from anxiety being the goal, the cravenness factor in cowardice is harder to find in anxiety disorders.

But cowardice may play a role in this sense. Avoidance behaviors can get so completely out of hand that failure to confront the problem borders closely on classic ideas of cowardice. Employment, family, even physical survival can be threatened by the disorder and the failure to deal with it is a form of running away from life. Over the long run the difference between the short-term release of anxiety and the long-term loss of a family or career provides the contrast needed to make the term more intelligible. Behavior becomes so dysfunctional that it is hard to justify not trying to do something about it. Modern drug therapies have gone a long way toward helping phobics and people with extreme anxiety. But the decision to seek help or not is still a *decision* and the process of psychological healing itself, even with drugs, is never decision-free. So perhaps, after all, use of the term "cowardice" can make some sense.

The philosopher Alasdair MacIntyre notes that we integrate our lives around meaningful projects ranging from marriage to career to hobbies.[3] Anxiety can make such life projects impossible to maintain. The person with a severe phobia is constantly on guard and cannot control his or her own destiny. A job perfectly suited for a person's skills may happen to be on the top floor of a building, so the job must be refused or the person soon quits. A potentially brilliant writer cannot research a book for fear of leaving the house. Our projects in life can be destroyed for many reasons, some of which, such as physical disasters or illness, we can do nothing about. But the person with a well-integrated mind can often go on and restructure a meaningful life even when personal tragedies strike. Reason can regain control. The individual with severe anxiety is hobbled in this regard from the beginning because part of his own mind is preventing rational integration around the goods of life. Courage is the most significant virtue in reintegrating the self and can be a catalyst toward providing the freedom to pursue the goals of life.

IRRATIONAL ANXIETY

The following account was written by an intelligent, professional woman who describes herself as suffering from a "phone phobia." That label is something of a misnomer because she is not anxious about the telephone but rather about the social interactions that take place on the phone.

"When I'm on the phone, I am extremely tense—it's as if I'm 'on the line,' and I am almost paralyzed with fear. I feel as though I have to justify making the call, have a good reason for calling so that I don't 'bother' the other person, and have to explain what I want clearly and briefly so as not to take up too much of the other person's time. I am always sure that I am going to make an ass of myself when I call someone.

"Over the years, I have developed certain strategies for dealing with my phone phobia. For any call, I establish a day and a time for making the call—it's on my calendar. However, I often postpone important calls if my level of tension is too high when they come up on my calendar. If I make the call and the other person is out, I am always relieved.

"I also feel threatened, tense, and anxious when I receive calls. I feel as if I'm being put on the spot, and I won't be able to think fast enough to come up with intelligent answers to the other person's questions. When the phone rings, I may start to tremble badly. To deal with my fear, I have established a firm rule for myself: I always pick up the phone after the second ring. With that rule, I give myself a little time to build up my courage, but I can't avoid the fear by not answering the phone. This phone phobia makes my professional and personal life really difficult. It's all rather crazy, but I can't get over it, so I just try to get around it."

Case cited in David Holmes, *Abnormal Psychology*, 2nd edition, 82

Irrational anxiety has many forms and millions of people structure their lives around irrational fears. For some people what begins as an anxious moment or a peculiar bodily reaction can, through a series of well-documented steps, become a full-blown panic attack.[4] My goal in this section is to explore some of the aspects of irrational anxiety and locate moments of psychological courage. Humans everywhere on the planet have real-life situations in which anxiety and panic have an objective and realistic foundation, ranging from the anxiety of giving a speech before strangers to the justifiable panic when the flooded river is rapidly approaching one's home. But the anxiety I will discuss below is not based on objective evidence or genuine threats. Looking at how and why irrational anxiety occurs may help people appreciate the courage it takes to deal with it.

Anxiety attacks, and their most extreme form, panic attacks, are episodes of intense fear and terror, accompanied by frightening bodily sensations and terrifying thoughts.[5] The bodily sensations include rapidly pounding heart, tightness in the chest and difficulty breathing. Dizziness, trembling, sweating and nausea are also common. The thoughts may include ideas of suffocating, dying, and completely losing control. Such attacks may have any number of original sources—a sudden anxiety about some location, a worrisome bodily change that has no medical explanation, a stressful relationship with a teenager you love—any number of possibilities. What builds the anxiety and panic is then a cycle of *remembering* locations and bodily feelings and an increasing fear of repeating those experiences.[6] Once extreme anxiety occurs the person may become hyper-aware of his own bodily sensations and what might be a mere passing anxiety to John becomes the sign of an incipient attack for Tom. As many writers have noted, full panic attacks are literally "fear of fear." As the cycle progresses, going near a grocery store may bring total panic or having a heart palpitation can paralyze a person with terror.

Anxiety and panic attacks are more extreme forms of irrational anxieties which almost all of us carry around in one degree or another. The stronger the anxiety, the less freedom we have to choose rationally the course of our lives. Those with wide-ranging and intense phobias or obsessions lead very constricted lives but all irrational anxiety constricts us to some extent. Irrational anxieties are associated with certain *assumptions* which reinforce the anxiety and certain *actions* taken which reduce the anxiety in the short run but which end up reinforcing it. These assumptions and avoidance behaviors are present in some degree in all cases of obsessive and irrational anxiety and understanding them can provide brief windows for psychological courage. Severe irrational or obsessive anxiety, unlike most cases of self-deception or self-justification, is a far more traumatic psychological experience and counseling or therapy is almost always useful or necessary. Without the guidance of a trusted counselor, courage in the face of powerful anxiety may be impossible.

Babior and Goldman analyze many of the assumptions and techniques used by people prone to anxiety.[7] In the remainder of this section I want to examine several of these points from the standpoint of psychological courage. Each of them represents a door through which a person must walk in order to grow. Without courage, and quite possibly the help of a trusted counselor or friend, a person will not be able to walk through these doors. I have phrased each one in the form of a positive character trait.

Admitting We Are Not Perfect

Perfectionism is a major assumption of people prone to anxiety and panic. This often takes the form of messages we give ourselves. For example, "Why can't I do this right" or "Why do I act so stupid" or, in response to a small error, "This is awful."[8] Perfectionistic people overgeneralize using the rule "I should never make mistakes." Such individuals may be quite successful yet seem to be unable to enjoy life. They say to themselves things like, "I had a fairly good week, but there was one afternoon when things didn't go very well."[9] This tendency, quite outside of its relationship to anxiety attacks, permeates much of the modern world where people are driven to succeed but are so insecure that they cannot take the time to enjoy what they have achieved. An obsession over perfectionism is one reason for misery by so many people in the midst of success.

The perfectionist is on a vicious downward cycle fueled by anxiety. When Joan does not reach her goals or when she fails, her muscles become tense, a sense of foreboding about the future grips her, and her mind automatically reverts to thoughts of worthlessness. After all, Joan's life is defined by being perfect, and she has failed. Her "self-talk" has been filled with self put-downs for not being perfect much of her life—it's habitual. And now she has reinforced that. She now tries harder, perhaps ups the goal even more, and fails again. Her self-talk becomes "What then am I worth?" Despite actually doing above average work, Joan has little or no joy in life. Courage lies in accepting her own imperfections as a person and, as Peurifoy puts it, "learning to enjoy being human."[10]

Psychological courage here is more than what we discussed in chapter one, i.e., overcoming the natural human tendency to defend our self-image. The admission in Joan's case runs counter to a deep personality trait of unforgiving perfection. This means coming to grips with intense anxiety. Techniques on how to do that are well-documented.[11] For example, practice rational and realistic self-talk while courageously facing the initial feelings of failure. (And those feelings can be intense). Set realistic goals while at the same time confronting the tendency you've developed of setting unrealistic ones. Recognize that realistic goals can be moved up incrementally and realistically and that failure is a learning process, not a statement about your self-worth. The heart of courage here means getting to the heart of the obsession. *Why* do you need to be a perfectionist? Why are you anxious when you cannot achieve what was not achievable? *That* fear is where the door to courage lies.

In the West achieving excellence is a fundamental goal. The ideal was first elaborated by the Greek philosophers, especially Aristotle, who argued that human happiness lies in the development of excellence.[12] Isn't there a contradiction here between striving for excellence and accepting "realistic goals?" If there is no obsession, there is no contradiction. Imagine running a marathon and coming in 389th place. You trained all year, loved it, and were hoping for a top 200 finish. As Aristotle (as well as modern psychologists) say, the process itself was central to your sense of fulfillment. This is as true in running as it is in teaching or building cabinets. But goals clearly are important too. You *did* want to finish higher. If you fail in the particular goal you set at the end but have done the best you can, accept that, but enjoy what is there to be enjoyed. Evaluate the goal, evaluate the process, evaluate where you want to put your time. Take it from there. But don't let the goal become an obsession which destroys the joy of getting there. Life is precious and enjoyment of our powers and abilities all too rare. Having the courage to face and overcome obsessive feelings of perfection is the first step to pursuing excellence and still enjoying each step along the way.

Giving Up Control When Appropriate

A second assumption permeated by anxiety is the belief that a person *must* be in control. We normally think courage is required to take control of a difficult situation. While this is often true, it also takes courage to give up control when that is appropriate. Cowardice is usually seen as a fear of being assertive, a fear of taking charge. But a person may demand control out of fear; in other words, the cowardly act may be refusing to give up control because of some anxiety. This is what the obsession about control is all about. It is not about maintaining control for a genuine good or for genuine efficiency. It is a fear of giving up control because the self will then be set adrift and we will have to lean on other people. Untrustworthy or uncaring parents or peers may have taught a person that giving up control is dangerous—that leaning on or trusting others is foolhardy. This "lesson" can be so deep as to instill anxiety in the person at even the thought of giving control to others. But, quite simply, that is not an accurate assessment of the world. There are definitely many people who cannot be trusted and yet many who can. Obsessive control governed by anxiety prevents us from making the distinction between the two.

But surely we all want to control our lives. What's wrong with that? The difference is that, when you give up control for rational reasons, *you* are the choice-maker in that decision and *you* reserve the right to change your mind. It is you who realize that the greater good will be served by being part of the team or letting someone with greater skill take charge. You are still the master of your own life because your reason is guiding your actions. But that is not the case with obsessive control. When anxiety forces you to be in control, there may or may not be benefits for the larger good; it is largely a matter of luck. Those in obsessive control must constantly prove they deserve that control and therefore may make rash or poorly reasoned decisions. After all, it is

not realism that guides their decisions; it is their personal need to avoid anxiety. The person in obsessive control will listen poorly because honest and
open listening is a form of letting go of our preconceptions and that creates
anxiety. People in obsessive control are cowards who are terrified of the different, the creative, the unique. Since all of these create anxiety, they are rejected by an obsessive controller with a terse response, phony excuses, or
simply avoidance.

Psychological courage lies in facing the question: *Why* do I need to control
everything? Why am I afraid of letting go? What, realistically, will happen if I
do listen and accept someone else's ideas or leadership? The obsessive controller must learn to confront and work through the anxiety produced by letting
go. Then, and only then, can a person be realistic about when she should be in
control and when it is best to listen and act under someone else's guidance.

Being Able to Accept Negative Feelings from Others

For millions of people a third assumption governed by anxiety is that everybody must like them. This assumption is about as realistic as the idea that a
person can control everything, yet it is a persistent idea in this consumer-
oriented society. Some people structure much of their existence around the
anxiety of potentially not being liked. A negative look, a hostile comment, a
bit of gossip—any of this can inflict a disturbing blow to our self-worth. So
these experiences must be avoided at all costs. The borders of such lives are
constantly patrolled by anxiety.

But again it is natural to want to be accepted by others. We *are* social beings. So what is the problem here? Once again the problem revolves around
a confusion between what is realistic for us socially and what we come to expect of ourselves irrationally. The courage to face negative reactions from
others means being able to accept yourself—your ideas, your actions, your relationships. Psychologically, it is healthier to be respected for integrity while
being disliked than it is simply to be liked at all costs. At the moment when
anxiety begins, ask yourself: Is being liked by this person worth the trade-off
required? How important is this individual to me? Does the other person have
any realistic grounds for his or her own views? Ultimately, you have to grit
your teeth and stand on your feet despite possible disapproval. That takes
guts.

Note that this is not stubbornness. Nothing in the above says that you ought
not take others' opinions seriously. But the rational person not driven by anxiety can ask herself whether the other person's perspective *should* be considered. Just as there is no virtue in trying to be liked all the time, there is no
virtue in deliberately affronting people. In the first case, anxiety about our

self-image keeps us from having integrity; in the second, anxiety about proving ourselves keeps us from growing through honest interaction with others. But the courageous and rational person, rational in both mind and emotional confidence, will allow herself to be disliked if honest thoughtful integrity is the only other alternative. Without obsessive anxiety about being liked, a person is so much more free to be honest with herself and others. If an act is virtuous under other lights—honest, thoughtful, responsible—and your honest judgment of others' negative reaction is that their views are not well-founded, hold your ground. Psychological courage is defeating the anxiety you will face.

Accepting My Worth as a Human Being

Related but somewhat different is the assumption driven by anxiety that I am a worthless or inferior person. Anxiety in this case leads to withdrawal or to constant efforts to "prove" oneself as worth something. Why would people feel this way? There are many possible reasons, e.g., consistent negative labeling or humiliation by parents or peers, physical or mental disabilities, social rejection. It has happened many times in history that people driven by the anxiety of being inferior have done great deeds. Irrational anxiety can have positive utilitarian results. But history also shows the opposite—people out to prove their worth were willing to do so by any means possible, often very destructive. (Napoleon would seem to be a classic example.) Perhaps everyone in one degree or another has some irrational sense of inferiority, at least in certain areas. The question is: how do we deal with it?

Withdrawal itself is a form of psychological cowardice. Certainly, as noted in chapter one, some people may be justified in doing this. Psychological and social pressures from childhood may be so intense as to make self-acceptance virtually impossible. But, for the majority, by the time we are adults and have some time to reflect on our lives, withdrawal cannot be automatically justified by our upbringing. Refusing to become involved in a relationship or career because of some sense of inferiority can become an easy way out, a way to avoid the anxiety of asserting oneself. The key again is to identify that moment of fear and turn it around. Why am I afraid? Can I overcome this sense of feeling inferior? Isn't life too short for this?

But is *overachieving* the rational opposite? No. Over-reacting to the anxiety is another way of avoiding the real issue, which is an internal one. How? David was frequently put down as a child for his weight. Whenever he thought about himself, he felt embarrassed and anxiety permeated his social relationships. David determined some time during adolescence that he was going to "show them." He went through high school with no social life but great grades and went on to college to get an honors degree in business. Still resentful inside and insecure and anxious socially, he entered the business world and moved up the ladder, using people and lying to them as necessary along the way. David entered a model marriage. He and his wife did not talk much at all about mutual feelings, joys, sorrows, or failings, but they had the ideal marriage for their careers. David made a great deal of money and was viewed as a great success. He had a wonderful public image but was still mad as hell inside.

Some version of this kind of story I think is quite common, at least in the Western world. But the hollowness inside cannot be filled by adding more and more baubles to the outside. Without facing the central anxiety and coming to grips with what obsessively drives us, everything we do has an ulterior motive. It is not "authentic," as the existentialist philosophers say. Genuine joy touches the soul, and the hollow laughter at "successful" parties cannot replace that. An honest, deep loving conversation in a marriage is worth untold number of false but wonderful social images. Without psychological courage in accepting ourselves as worthy and secure human beings, our achievements, though possibly very important socially, cannot do away with the anxiety. Our successes will be covers that end up in the worst cases never being satisfying and never enough.

Do courage and self-acceptance then lead to mediocrity? Isn't obsessiveness necessary for greatness? No. Why is there a "necessary" contradiction between accepting your strengths and weaknesses and doing great things? If a person truly loves music or business or engineering, why can't the person make some choices, choices made with the conscious realization of likely results? Is it not better to *choose* a career over marriage (or vice-versa) rather than to have achievement be an obsession? Loving a career or loving a person can lead to noble achievements without the ulterior motive of being driven to prove oneself. Self-acceptance can lead to "owning" achievements in a more deeply satisfying way. Whether in business or music or architecture, greatness in a field is independent of how one achieves it, yet how one *experiences* those achievements has everything to do with that intimate self-acceptance only possible though courageously accepting ourselves.

Thinking Objectively and Realistically

A common reaction to anxiety in all forms is called "catastrophic thinking" which means a tendency to think the worst of a situation. For the perfectionist it might be: "I can never do this right" or for the obsessive controller: "If I am not in control, things will go down the tubes." The deeper the anxiety, the more prominent this type of thinking. For people with frequent panic attacks, catastrophic thoughts are everywhere. The mere sight of a certain building or person, a simple bodily sensation, a memory—any of them can stimulate catastrophic thoughts about total social embarrassment, an impending heart attack, or feeling trapped. People will often justify their fears by reading about or listening to examples which support their catastrophic ideas—airline disasters, for example. This reinforces the idea that the world is uncontrollable and catastrophes are likely.[13] The anxiety channels and drives our thoughts toward negative images which reinforce the anxiety.

This makes courage a central issue in turning catastrophic thinking into rational thoughts. How? Many books dealing with anxiety do an excellent job of talking about techniques to promote rational thinking, i.e. ways of substituting for a catastrophic thought one based on evidence and actual experience.[14] And counselors dealing with anxiety and panic are trained in these techniques. As effective as these techniques are, there is one facet that rests solely on the shoulders of the client—dealing with moments of anxiety *as they arise*. And awareness of catastrophic thinking can be important at these moments.

Very often we are not consciously aware of immediate feelings; they often are so habitual that they fall below the level of conscious awareness. When a catastrophic thought arises, its origin lies in the pit of anxiety. With the help of a counselor or through deep self-reflection, catch that thought. That will help make you aware of the root anxiety. Then comes a moment of courage. Substituting a rational thought for a catastrophic one is not just an intellectual exercise. It is a gut-wrenching, courageous act. We are giving up a safety net. The catastrophic thought is a way of insuring that the safety net remains. For example, anxiety may be linked to the catastrophic thought, "If I don't take responsibility, nobody else will," which leads to "So I better take over again," which in turn lessens anxiety. But this safety net, "taking over again," is a short-term, unrealistic and energy-draining fraud. The self-talk and exposure techniques used by many anxiety counselors can go a long way toward realism and living without the net. But the choice is still yours and the moments of anxiety, so habituated over time, must still be faced and overcome.

Though this is not primarily a book about therapeutic techniques, I want to close this section with an example given by Peurifoy that spells out in more detail what the steps are in overcoming catastrophic thinking. And I would like the reader to take a second at each sentence break in here and think about the *emotions* that must be faced and think about how easy it would be to slide back into the habitual anxiety pattern.

Example: Pat is a shipping clerk who has sent a shipment to the wrong location. She catches herself dwelling on how she is worthless and always makes a mess of things.

Pat's rational self-talk: "Wait a minute. I am not a worthless screw-up! I am simply a human being who has made a mistake (substitution) . . . Actually, I'm a very good worker who is just as accurate and productive as the other clerks (ego strengtheners). Now, exactly what went wrong? It seems I punched the wrong code into the computer when I coded the address labels (objective evaluation). I guess the first thing I need to do is make sure that shipment gets re-routed. Then I can figure out how it got mixed up (redirecting statements)."[15]

First is an acceptance of her humanity—being able to forgive herself. To accept that she is "simply a human being who has made a mistake" means facing the anxiety that she is not perfect—she does not meet her own or some others' ideas of perfection. Difficult to do when you have hinged your self-identity on an unrealistic idea of perfection. To give that up means giving up part of one's old "self." Second is the acceptance of her strengths. This means overcoming a certain amount of self-pity—to be worthless and have no strengths is a self-pitying excuse and, with that excuse, Pat does not then have to deal with reality. This is a peculiar but very common phenomenon. We get anxious about failing and then can get a type of self-centered high about thinking how worthless we are—a type of "poor me" syndrome. (This might fit well the old Freudian idea of "fixation" at a childhood level. It is typical childhood and early adolescent behavior.) Accepting that she is "as accurate and productive as the other clerks" and *believing* that takes courage since sliding into anxiety–induced self-pity is so much easier. Once Pat gets to step 3—objective evaluation—she will have made some progress in facing down the anxiety of worthlessness or else there would *be* no "objective" evaluation. At this point and at point four—redirecting statements—factors discussed in chapter one take more precedence. If she has overcome or at least partially overcome the irrational anxiety of failure, then she has to face the more everyday problems of self-justification and self-honesty. OK now, did I punch that wrong code in? If I did, was it maybe because my co-worker talks too much or maybe because the codes are so similar that it's the system's fault? Issues about bridging cognitions (I am a good worker vs. I made a fairly large mistake) or self-pretense (I'm not responsible because the system is at fault) become dominant issues of courage. It is possible to view the self-talk of worthlessness as a way of reducing dissonance and a form of self-deception. (After all, if I am worthless, the first cognition is reduced.) However, the dominance of obsessive anxiety early on calls for a variation of psychological courage not present in everyday forms of self-justification. No one wants to confront a negative self-image but not all are driven by anxiety toward perfection, a need for total control, or overdependence.

Being Aware of Avoidance Techniques

A common way to avoid irrational anxiety is simply to stay away from places, people or thoughts which produce the anxiety. So Michael avoids the airport where he experienced an anxiety attack, Debra avoids her boss because she cannot handle authority figures well at all, and Tom avoids thoughts about sex because he gets so anxious and guilty it disrupts his life. The paradoxical part of all this is that the research on anxiety indicates that the more a person does this, the more it strengthens the anxiety. By avoiding these situations, it heightens sensitivity to them and strengthens the fear of having anxiety. This is yet another vicious cycle.[16] Anxiety about a place leads to avoiding the place which intensifies the fear of having the anxiety in these circumstances and then increases the likelihood of avoidance. Moreover, such places, people and ideas have a radiating effect in our mind. Anxiety about sex leads to avoiding sexual thoughts which intensifies the fear of having the anxiety and makes Tom hyper-sensitive to the thoughts. It now is not just thoughts of sex but thoughts that are associated with sex that must be avoided. Or it is not just the airport but other forms of transportation which can, after all, have some of the same dangers as flying.

Overcoming avoidance is one of the clearest cases of psychological courage. Counselors will use exposure techniques in both imagination and real life to help a client overcome the fear.[17] They will, for example, have a client imagine himself going through the different stages of an airport check-in. The therapist then may accompany the client to the airport door, then next session to the check-in line, etc. In other cases, the therapist might help the client imagine herself independent of her parents, then as a "homework" lesson fill out a college application, then take a trip out of town, etc. But in all these the heart of success lies in the courage of the individual herself to go through the exposure process. No matter how incrementally done, the person must still face the anxiety. Until and unless drugs can directly manipulate brain chemistry and make anxiety completely susceptible to immediate cure, a person will have to make *decisions*. With anxiety over physical or psychological annihilation, those decisions will involve courage.

Knowing What We Are Doing and Why We Are Doing It

The last trait I want to discuss is the tendency to avoid anxiety by mindless actions which take our mind off it. How many people in this society talk, drink, eat or do any number of things simply to avoid anxiety? A broad term for this phenomenon is displacement. Desmond Morris, the biologist who has written on the comparative behavior of humans and others primates, notes that at parties, especially parties where we do not want to be, we will often feel quite anxious. In order to distract from that anxiety, we do what Morris calls displacement drinking (everyone carries around a drink to sip when necessary) and displacement eating (that's what hors d'oeuvres are for, even if we are not hungry).[18] We also do a great deal of displacement talking. The latter, as a form of distraction from anxiety, is one reason why we cannot remember the content of such conversations seconds after they occur. The point was not to carry on an actual conversation but to relieve mutual anxiety.

While everyone goes through times like this and more or less accepts the social conventions that allay anxiety, people driven by obsessive anxiety are less fortunate. When we leave that party (or that conference or that speech class), we generally leave the anxiety behind. Memories of past anxiety are flashes of lightning too distant to worry about. But the person with obsessive anxiety cannot leave it behind. Therefore, his or her acts of distraction take on a driven, encompassing characteristic. Joann may spend a lot of time at work because she loves her job or needs the money. Or she might spend a lot of time at work because she does not want to *stop* working. If she does, she may have to deal with the anxiety of feeling inferior socially. Joe spends a great deal of time at the bar drinking his way over his dependency anxiety and Ruth distracts herself from the anxiety of perfectionism by playing games of chance, lots of them. Much of this could be classified under self-deception as a form of "systematic distraction." The difference here, and it is a matter of degree, is that obsessive anxiety drives the person to distraction. That is why counseling is so fundamental because, in the cauldron of fear, we need a hand to lift us out far enough to get perspective and facilitate courage.

As noted above, the actual results of distraction or obsessive behavior may be impressive. Obsessiveness over perfection can kill the joy of stamp or coin collecting but it sure can produce a beautiful collection. Distraction at work may keep Joann from ever dealing with her deep anxiety about social inferiority but, wow, the quality and quantity of her work is first-rate. But a tragic element lurks below the surface. Given the shortness of one's life, a person should have some say about what he or she would rationally choose to do with that life. Being driven around by anxiety wastes our all-too-precious moments on earth. Being aware of what we are doing and why we are doing it is the first step. Then, if anxiety raises its head as a driving force, we can hopefully notice that fact, face the fear, work through it, and do creative or useful work in what we choose to do because we find it fulfilling. I know this is ideal, and the social system itself with all its pressures may militate against it, but a life of psychological freedom, free from the fear-driven and energy-wasting actions of obsessive and irrational anxiety, should be the birthright of every human being, not a select few. For all of us courage is one important ingredient in getting there.

THE WISDOM OF THE STOICS

What upsets people is not things themselves but their judgments about the things. . . . So when we are thwarted or upset or distressed, let us never blame someone else but rather ourselves, that is, our own judgments.

Epictetus, *The Handbook of Epictetus*, translated by Nicholas P. White, 13

The ancient Stoic philosophers may seem to have little to do with facing anxiety except perhaps in a negative sense. They are often interpreted, with some good reason, as denying or repressing anxiety rather than facing it and their strength seems to lie in having physical courage in the face of death. For example, as is well known, Vice Admiral James Stockdale credits the Stoics with helping him survive eight years as a prisoner of war in North Vietnam, four years in solitary confinement. Epictetus, one of the major figures in Stoicism, was a slave who had his leg broken by his master and who accepted and developed Stoicism when he gained his freedom partly because of that experience. But there is more to Stoicism than just being, well, stoic. And some of the points they raise are highly relevant to anyone trying to deal with anxiety.

First, a brief overview of Stoicism. The Stoics claim that we have little or no control over most things that happen to us in life. The universe works as it does independent of our wishes. Hurricanes, earthquakes, diseases and bad genes affect the lives of millions. Likewise, the thoughts and actions of other people are almost always beyond our control. The drunk driver who just happens to be on the road at the same time as your child, your incompetent boss who keeps his job because of connections with the owner, your neighbor who resents your success in life—all of them we have little or no control over. Granted, we have come a long way in controlling nature from the time of the Stoics 2000 years ago. We no longer have to sit passively by while disease wipes out our family and, even for events we cannot directly control, we have some measure of prediction. Yet cancer, earthquakes and slippery roads in winter remind us that we are still prone to nature's whims. As far as other people go, we have made some progress in understanding why people do the things they do and we have found some very limited ability to control some of the most destructive human actions, yet, all in all, the thoughts and actions of other people are as unpredictable and uncontrollable today as they were in 100 AD for Epictetus. In fact, with the current population pressures and the anonymity of large cities, people's thoughts and actions related to us may well be less predictable.

Given all this, how do we respond? A key point of the Stoics is that most people waste an enormous amount of their lives being resentful, hostile, or frustrated over events that are already completed or over which they have no control. What you are doing in these cases is *giving your life away* to the event or person. You buy a new car and park it carefully in an out-of-the-way part of the parking lot. At some point during the day a joy-riding bunch of teenagers, thinking about other things, sideswipe your new car causing considerable damage. Many people would not only be upset at the incident, they would be upset for a long time and develop thoughts to match their frustration (perhaps about teenagers or teen drivers). Then, whenever a similar situation arises or even the thought, the initial frustration gets renewed. Millions of people have axes to grind, abiding resentments, and chips on their shoulders because of real or imagined slights. But the Stoics ask some simple questions: Why are you allowing someone else to dictate your life? Why waste the precious moments you have in useless and irritating emotions over events that are either past in time or over which you have no control? Why give your freedom of thought and expression to some long-gone teenage driver (or, far more seriously, to the torturer in front of you)? Maintain your freedom. Your life is your own.

Two points here especially stand out as relevant for psychological courage. First is the preciousness of the moments we have. One of the most striking characteristics of obsessive anxiety is the amount of time and energy it takes up. People who feel undesirable socially will spend much of their lives avoiding experiences where that anxiety will occur. Their lives are constrained by a series of "nots"—not there, not with that person, not that job. If you are in that situation, you are basically forfeiting your life. You have given control of your life to your anxiety. At least the Stoics talk about real events like accidents and diseases. But you have given up your freedom to a bunch of negative fantasies, images created by your mind which reinforce the anxiety of being unacceptable. Even if there is some sort of pleasure of self-pity involved in this, the Stoics would be quite blunt: how incredibly sad, what a wasted life.

Remember that the Stoics were not therapists and empathy was not part of their mode of expression. For the Stoics slavery, poverty, starvation and death were all around them. They would have little sympathy for modern psychological problems when physical illness and death were always around the next corner. Unlike some other Stoics, Epictetus knew the uncertainties and terrors of life very personally. He beautifully puts the Stoic point about the ever-present potential of death:

> On a voyage when your boat has anchored, if you want to get fresh water you may pick up a small shellfish and a vegetable by the way, but you must keep your mind fixed on the boat and look around frequently in case the captain calls. If he calls you must let all those other things go so that you will not be tied up

and thrown on the ship like livestock. That is how it is in life too: if you are given a wife and a child instead of a vegetable and a small shellfish, that will not hinder you; but if the captain calls, let all those things go and run to the boat without turning back; and if you are old, do not even go very far from the boat, so that when the call comes you are not left behind.[19]

Though we may have a few more years on the voyage, the captain calls us just as surely as Epictetus. And perhaps if we keep that in mind it might help motivate courage to take control of our lives from the grip of anxiety.

The second major point I want to raise about the Stoics is their emphasis on your decisions about your emotional state. This is very different from the way we think today. At one point Epictetus says, "Remember that what is insulting is not the person who abuses you or hits you, but the judgment about them that they *are* insulting. So when someone irritates you be aware that what irritates you is your own belief."[20] So, if someone steps on your foot and you get angry, your anger is your *choice*. You are in fact free to respond any way you like.

Now this startling claim is hard to buy for several reasons. First, it completely ignores habits that may be so deep as to be out of awareness. Children who are treated in an abusive way for a long time do not have choices; patterns of response can be laid down long before there is any conscious awareness of options. Moreover, the Stoic claim seems to fly in the face of biological fact—we have certain responses to situations (like being struck) that have nothing to do with choice. And, finally, it seems to be bad psychological advice in general. If I have someone irritating me for no good reason and I do not respond emotionally, those feelings of resentment do not just disappear. They often tend to fester and promote the very thing we are trying to overcome—irritation or anxiety.

But, granted those significant provisos, the Stoic point contains a great deal of truth that is largely ignored today. They even have responses to the examples above. Not all abused children grow up to be abusive; choices can still be made. A natural biological response can be checked at certain points; we are not slaves to biology. And there are more options when it comes to expressing emotions than simply repressing them or mindlessly giving into them. That is a false dilemma. In general, we make a far too easy assumption today that our emotions and responses depend on other people or situations. Our obsession with being accepted and lovable makes us slaves to the views of others, especially advertising and mass marketing. And our highly pleasure-oriented society, which always talks of freedom, may actually block it. The Stoics say that people who are hedonists—pleasure-seekers—have given up their freedom to whatever pleasure happens to be in front of them at the moment. Freedom means responsibility of personal choice and there is an inverse relationship between the ability to choose our life and the degree to which we are led around by our emotions and desires. I am not advocating the Stoic extreme about emotions here. Epictetus and other Stoics often sound cold and far too aloof from the pain around them and they seem to get little joy out of life. Nevertheless, I believe the fundamental Stoic point is a powerful one—if you *realize* your thoughts, actions and responses are literally yours to decide, you may find you actually *have* more options in real life.

Dealing with irrational anxiety fits well at this point. When you become aware of moments of anxiety or negative assumptions or actions, *stop*, if but a second. (Again a good counselor can help at these times). *You* have control over your thoughts, actions, and yes, to some degree, your emotions. And you may find that, as you modify your thoughts and actions, your emotions will change too. It is somewhat analogous to being in a car accident that is not your fault. Assuming the accident is not severe, the initial biological response will probably be anger toward the other driver. But catch yourself a moment after that instinctive response. The accident is done, over with. What good will your expression of anger do? What good will angry actions achieve? Very likely, not much, and it will probably make a bad situation worse. In some cases in life, anger may be a teaching tool for another person; in many cases, not. There are, as Aristotle noted, appropriate amounts of anger in different circumstances.[21] But those amounts are governed by a sense of what we call today maturity, a sense of overall rational control of one's life. Applied back to anxiety, there are plenty of moments that justify anxiety in life in one degree or another—from the upcoming speech to a missing child. But irrational and obsessive anxiety is not an appropriate response to reality, it is, pure and simple, *your* invention. As such, with help as needed, you can take your freedom back. And, when life throws at us what we really cannot control, you may find that your freedom gives you options you never dreamed you had.

THE BUDDHIST RESPONSE TO ANXIETY

The biggest obstacle to taking a bigger perspective on life is that our emotions capture and blind us. The more sensitive we become to this, the more we realize that when we start getting angry or denigrating ourselves or craving things in a way that makes us feel miserable, we begin to shut down, shut out, as if we were sitting on the edge of the Grand Canyon but we had put a big black bag over our heads.

You can experiment with this. You can go out there to the cliffs overlooking the Gulf of Saint Lawrence, and the first hit is always, "Wow! It's so big," and your mind opens. But if you stand there long enough, you'll start to worry about something. Then you realize (if you want to do this as an exercise) that it feels as if everything is closing down and getting very small. The trick about nowness is that you can let go and open up again to that space. You can do that at any moment, always. But it does take making friends with yourself. It does take coming to know your anger, coming to know your self-deprecation, coming to know your craving and wanting, coming to know your boredom, and making friends with those things.

Pema Chödrön, The Wisdom of No Escape, 30–31

Courage for the Stoic is a decision not to give up your freedom, i.e., not to allow either external or internal forces to drive your life irrationally. Put positively, courage is a decision to take control of your actions in cases in which you have control of them and, when you don't, to maintain inner control of your responses to the world around you. I want to close this chapter with a different approach to dealing with anxiety that applies courage in a different way. For the Buddhist, dealing with anxiety is less a function of decision than it is of awareness. Levels of awareness are also critical in the West and almost all forms of therapy for anxiety (with the possible exception of the purist behavioral therapy) combine awareness with changes in behavior. But in Buddhism that awareness runs to new depths and indeed constitutes the heart of what life is about. For the Buddhist it would make no sense to say "I have really bad dependence anxiety." Rather, when you are in that state, you *are* dependence anxiety.

Boldly put, the Buddhist does not think there is a self. The self is an illusion created when various "parts" work together. The Buddha's own example is a chariot. What is a "chariot" except a composite of parts functioning in a certain way? There is no permanent thing called "chariot." In the same way there is no permanent thing called "I." Our ego sense develops when the parts (called "skandhas" in Buddhism) function together—inner sensations, outer perceptions, consciousness, physical body, mental formulations.[22] If one of those dominates, then that part is the main source of the "ego" at that time. Language forces us to think objectively about ourselves. For example, if I am enthralled by the stars in the night sky, language states it as "*I* am enthralled by the night sky." But, the Buddhists say, if "you" (language again) are truly enthralled by the sight, then "you" as a separate ego have momentarily ceased to exist. Before criticizing the Buddhists on their view of self, think a moment about this experience. If you truly are absorbed in an experience like a poem, a conversation, or the night sky, what *are* you at that moment? As soon as "I" step back in and start saying things like "Wow, I think that sky is beautiful," I have already distanced myself from the experience and am back in the ego of ideas. The Buddhists claim that the most joyous experiences we have in this life are when we can get rid of this false "ego." If you are in a conversation, lose yourself in it. If you are reading a poem, lose yourself in it. In other words, whatever the reality is you are engaged in, lose that nagging concern we have about protecting this illusion of self.

Obsessive anxiety is a deep form of ego protectiveness which effectively blocks people from merging with the reality around them. You cannot experience the joy of a shared relationship if you feel you *must* be in control or *must* take responsibility for everything or *must* depend on another person. All of those are ways of patrolling the bounds of the ego, so to speak. Courage comes in admitting to awareness the reality around us, including the vast amount of unnecessary psychological suffering. Psychological cowardice to the Buddhist would be living in fear of being fully aware. Most of us live that way much of the time; the obsessively anxious person has an added burden of terror.

One popular writer on Zen, Charlotte Joko Beck, has several points that tie into this. Two closely related ideas she discusses are "emotion-thoughts" and what she calls the "superstructure."[23] Imagine a relationship you are currently in—with a spouse, friend, boss, whatever. Beck claims, and I believe this is correct, that the vast majority of people do not actually live in those relationships but live in a "superstructure" built on top of the real world. So, for example, if I am currently relating to my spouse, my superstructure might be a composite of resentment, future expectations, stereotyped responses and unresolved conflicts. In other words, I am not dealing *now* with my spouse; I am relating to a mental construct, heavily influenced by emotions ("emotion thoughts") which will dictate my actions unless my awareness increases to tear down the superstructure. No one is talking about making the past or future irrelevant. But the past and future are not where you are. And to tear down that superstructure—to increase awareness of the present reality—is scary. It is just so much easier to live in the secure world of stereotypes and emotional ruts, to protect our precious ego from the reality around us. Courage is a constant process needed to keep awareness current and to stop protecting our grand illusion, the ego.

The way Beck puts it is that we need to practice living on "the razor's edge."[24] Her own path to this is Zen meditation but every person must find his or her own way. The key is to have some path, some technique, to block the power of emotion-thoughts and to break through the superstructure, that is, to reduce anxiety about the past and the future and the thoughts derived from that. It might be time with music or some hobby; it might be spending time in meditation or in prayer; it might be a relationship with someone—a spouse, friend or counselor—who insists on no B.S. and pushes you to be honest. All of them can help you become "a bigger container."[25] Any serious Buddhist will tell you that this is not easy. It takes self-discipline, honesty and, above all, courage to push our awareness out of the ruts, release our hold on the ego, and stop living in fear.

We are all in different situations. But, as another superb Buddhist writer, Pema Chödrön, says, it does not matter what you are given. You have to take what you have and do the best you can with it to *wake up*.[26] From the Buddhist perspective those who suffer from severe anxiety or an "uncontrollable" temper go through life half-asleep—their awareness of the rich possibilities around them continually blocked by fear or anger. Greater awareness allows us to reach what Beck labels the "cut-off point."[27] When anxiety or anger do arise, we can cut it off, not in the Stoic sense of a decision, but by overwhelming it, so to speak, with awareness of what we are doing and what is at hand. By increasing awareness, we can break free of the thoughts and emotions which bind us to some imagined sense of "ego" and can actually become one with the world around us.

Americans, not prone to meditation, often poke fun at this "becoming one" idea. It smacks of intellectual mushiness and lacks logical content. Yet those same Americans go on a vacation, take their anxieties with them, and then wonder why they didn't enjoy nature more. Or they drive themselves to make more money, buy numerous goods, and wonder why that second boat hasn't brought genuine contentment to their lives. At the same time many of those same people can lose themselves in the smile of a child, get so absorbed in a book that they forget about time, or find themselves in a genuine conversation with a close friend that they will remember forever. Despite such positive experiences we, who so easily put the Buddhists down, ignorantly keep telling ourselves that the anxiety-driven experiences in our lives are "reality." But perhaps the Buddhists are, in fact, right. Loss of ego puts us in touch with the real and giving up the false ego to achieve that greater awareness is an act of courage.

So now we have the West and the East. The Stoics say that overcoming anxiety is fundamentally a *decision* you make about your freedom, a decision about controlling your life grounded in the fragility and shortness of human existence. This decision seems to be a strong reinforcement of the self—the ultimate acknowledgment of the self's freedom to choose. But the Buddhists say that overcoming anxiety is a function of *awareness*, not any superficial intellectual awareness but the profound awareness of the falseness of the ego. Rather than the self making important decisions about freedom, this "self" is the problem. Are they contradictory? Certainly the Buddhists seem contradictory by stressing the meditation techniques "you" can use to abolish the illusion of "you." But their argument is that this is a linguistic problem and that reality is far richer and less permanent than our linguistic constructs. The question of whether there is a permanent self is a central one for what is called in philosophy "metaphysics," but I do not think it is central for our purposes here. Perhaps the Stoic "decision" could be viewed as a natural outgrowth of increasing awareness of reality and the increasing Buddhist "awareness" as another way of looking at steps toward a decision regarding reality. In any case, what I wanted to give the reader were two options for approaching irrational anxiety. Both are highly insightful. Both approaches require psychological courage, one a decision to be in control of our lives in the face of external and internal forces which would deny our freedom, the other the courage to move beyond false ego needs fed by fear to untested but time-transcending experiences that can change lives. I will leave the metaphysical issue to the reader. Suffice it to say that each is a helpful and effective way to view courage in the face of anxiety.

NOTES

1. David Holmes, *Abnormal Psychology*, 2nd edition (New York: Harper Collins, 1994), chapters 1–6; Christopher Peterson, *The Psychology of Abnormality* (New York: Harcourt Brace, 1996), chapter 7.

2. See Donald Goodwin, *Anxiety* (Oxford: Oxford University Press, 1986) for a good summary of anxiety's causal effect on behavior.

3. Alasdair MacIntyre, *After Virtue*, 2nd edition (Notre Dame: University of Notre Dame Press, 1984), chapter 15.

4. Reneau Peurifoy, *Anxiety, Phobias, and Panic* (New York: Warner Books, 1995), 17–19.

5. Peurifoy, *Anxiety*, 2.

6. Peurifoy, *Anxiety*, 17–19; Shirley Babior and Carol Goldman, *Overcoming Panic, Anxiety and Phobias* (Duluth, Minnesota: Whole Person Associates, Inc. 1996), 11–14; C.B. Serignar, *From Panic to Peace of Mind* (Gretna, Louisiana: Wellness Institute, 1991), chapter 2.

7. Babior and Goldman, *Overcoming Panic*, 66–69, 75–77. I am indebted to Babior and Goldman throughout this section for their concise and clear discussion of the assumptions and "security moves" accompanying anxiety.

8. Peurifoy, *Anxiety, Phobias, and Panic*, 127–28.

9. Peurifoy, *Anxiety*, 134–35.

10. Peurifoy, *Anxiety*, 126.

11. See Holmes, *Abnormal Psychology*, chapter 6, for a summary of treatment techniques for anxiety and references to studies about their efficacy. The books cited above—Babior and Goldman, Peurifoy, Serignar—restate and apply some of the most effective of those techniques.

12. Aristotle, *Nicomachean Ethics*, trans. J.A.K. Thomson, revised by Hugh Tredennick (London: Penguin Books, 1976), Books 1 and 2.

13. Babior and Goldman, *Overcoming Panic, Anxiety and Phobias*, 76.

14. See the books cited above. The best of these books on the market rely on accumulated evidence in clinical psychology.

15. Peurifoy, *Anxiety, Phobias, and Panic*, 100.

16. See Babior and Goldman, *Overcoming Panic*, 76.

17. The therapeutic exposure process is clearly laid out by Babior and Goldman, *Overcoming Panic*, 81–106, and by Peurifoy, *Anxiety*, 174–202. In the future virtual reality may play a useful role here.

18. Desmond Morris, *The Naked Ape* (New York: McGraw-Hill, 1967), 169–70.

19. Epictetus, *The Handbook of Epictetus*, trans. Nicholas P. White (Indianapolis: Hackett Publishing Co., 1983), 13.

20. Epictetus, *Handbook*, 16.

21. Aristotle, *Nicomachean Ethics*, Book 4.

22. See Nancy Wilson Ross, *Buddhism: A Way of Life and Thought* (New York: Vintage Books, 1980), 28–30.

23. Charlotte Joko Beck, *Everyday Zen: Love and Work* (New York: Harper-Collins, 1989), 71–73, 136-44.

24. Beck, *Everyday Zen*, 155–162.

25. Beck, *Everyday Zen*, 49–52.

26. Pema Chödrön, *The Wisdom of No Escape and the Path of Loving—Kindness* (Boston: Shambhala Publications, 1991), 27–32.

27. Beck, *Everyday Zen*, 56-64.

Chapter Three

Psychological Courage
and Social Relationships

PSYCHOLOGICAL CONTROL

Kathy described her own role in her family as that of a good, obedient daughter. Throughout her life she had always looked to her parents for advice and had rarely made a decision independently, even as late as college. Her parents were also very strict with her throughout her college years. Kathy described several instances of her parents' control. Kathy's parents chose her college and graduate school for her. They gave her a midnight curfew when she was home on vacations, and they also imposed a curfew on her when she was at school. Kathy recalled the time when she was a junior in college and her parents wouldn't allow her to attend any sorority parties because they would "keep her out too late." Kathy continued to honor this curfew throughout college and graduate school, even though both institutions were several hundred miles from her parents' home and such a curfew could not be enforced.

Kathy remained dependent on her parents' approval after school. For example, Kathy began to develop ambivalent feelings about Tom in the months before their wedding, yet she decided to get married anyway because her parents "had gone to a lot of trouble planning the wedding and I didn't want to disappoint them." . . .

Casebook in Abnormal Psychology, 3rd edition, edited by John Vitkus, 102–3.

One of the assumptions discussed in the previous chapter was the obsessive need to be in control and the courage it takes to give up control when appropriate. Here I want to approach the issue from the other side, that of the person controlled, and generalize the role of courage beyond overcoming obsessive anxiety. Humans are masters at controlling each other through emotional manipulation and the goal of manipulation can range from altruistic to cruel. Charities evoke pity and promote donations by showing needy or abandoned children on television. Advertisers compete to produce commercials that can better manipulate the emotions of the public. And a great deal of manipulation occurs in interpersonal relationships. To some extent every relationship involves some degree of emotional manipulation. There is nothing evil in itself about this—evoking emotional responses from one another is part of the dance of our life. But all too often emotional manipulation is destructive in a relationship. A couple that continually pulls each other's emotional strings as a way to "get" the other person can easily become trapped in a fruitless game of one-upmanship, a painful and frustrating way to spend one's years together. But that does not have to happen. Another couple may be aware of each other's emotional control mechanisms, talk about them, and recognize the other's emotional needs with knowledge and love. Attempts to manipulate can become an object of genuine warmth and humor between loving couples. In the best of cases both partners can learn and grow from the emotional dance that occurs in their relationship.

Beginning with the courage to be an independent human being, I want to explore in this chapter several aspects of psychological courage in human relationships. The chapter will examine some of the reasons we give for allowing ourselves to be controlled and why we refuse to act in situations which clearly call for courageous action. It will also look at the way we try to control situations by the judgments we make about other people and how courage in admitting our weaknesses can go a long way toward improving and enjoying social interaction.

Emotional control in a relationship has many forms and the motives of the controlling person play an important role in analyzing courage. In some cases the control may be quite innocent. A young man may be very attached to his older brother whose judgments profoundly affect the younger person's life. If such an effect is not promoted by the older brother, breaking away toward independence may be as much a matter of awareness of responsibility as courage. Courage will still be necessary to face the difficulties of life on his own and that may involve a difficult series of decisions. The older brother, however, is not a source of fear.

Another possibility is that a parent may enjoy having her older child do what the parent wants. The parent, unlike the older brother discussed above, is aware of her effect on the child and enjoys it. However, she does not intend to hold onto the child. When and if the child does choose her own way, the parent will agree. Courage by the child in this case involves, again, facing the world on her own, but it also might involve making her mother unhappy. Since genuine caring may exist all around in such a case, courage can be more difficult. It includes the recognition that facing life for the good of her own future may necessarily bring a sense of loss to someone who loves her.

A third possibility, and the model case for courage in this setting, is when one individual intends to control another. Classic cases are parents who do not want to let adult children lead their own lives, a spouse who controls the life of the other, or a religious cult leader who controls his members. Courage in all these cases means dealing with significant and justifiable fears. Physical dangers may be present. A woman confronting an abusive husband has to face her own anxieties about independence and decision-making along with the physical danger the husband may present. A young man breaking away from manipulative parents may endanger his life's financial security while at the same time facing fears about being independent. Moral principles may also blend in. Confronting a religious cult leader on whom one has become dependent may mean standing up for moral principles at the risk of social ostracism by the group, and this may be combined with the need to deal with personal anxieties about independent living and self-esteem.

The cultural background of the individual may play a significant role in how he or she perceives a situation of control. Consider marriage and the family. Our culture has historically emphasized honoring parents, sometimes at all costs, and remaining in a marriage, no matter how destructive it might be, is still an important value in some subcultures. For example, a person may be raised to believe that divorce will result in eternal damnation and even the most controlling or abusive marriage is better than an eternity of pain. A life of misery now will be nothing compared to the bliss of an eternal reward. Culture can thus play a big role in determining what options a person perceives herself to have and courage in these situations must be filtered through cultural barriers. Another complicating factor is positive caring by the person being controlled. The example in the previous paragraph of the young adult with the controlling parents points this out. The young man may genuinely care about his parents and may not want to see them hurt. While it may be true that much of his life is being crushed by parents who have no intention of voluntarily letting go, a judgment of cowardice in this case must be cautiously made.

Nevertheless, cultural and psychological preconditions never completely absolve people of responsibility for their own lives. Even in tightly controlled subcultures, moments of courage within an abusive marriage, for example, still exist. While divorce may be out of the question, a wife may defiantly defend her children or courageously speak to her husband about his anger. The barriers set by the culture do not eliminate the need for courageous choices. Similarly, the love or concern that a controlled child has for his parents does not eliminate the value of psychological courage. Those who have defended their personal rights against controlling or abusive spouses or parents speak to the critical importance of courage in cases of psychological control.[1] And, where courage is a live option, so is cowardice.

Cowardice can be covered up in such situations by self-deception. As noted in chapter one, self-deception as a front for cowardice can occur in substance-abuse disorders, e.g., the alcoholic who convinces himself that he has no problem in order to avoid dealing with the habit. But it can also occur in cases of emotional control. People can convince themselves that they are incapable of making autonomous decisions or living independent lives.[2] The person who claims love as the reason not to confront a controlling parent or abusive spouse may have convinced herself contrary to the evidence that control is a form of caring and submitting to that control is reciprocal love.[3] In situations of psychological control deceiving the self as a front for cowardice is easy to do. The safety of certain aspects of the situation allows an individual to put herself to sleep about the destructive elements. Self-deception prevents an accurate judgment of the facts of a situation, thus covering up any requirement to act. Acting courageously can be avoided by convincing ourselves we do not have a problem or by systematically ignoring what the problem is.

Like cowardice, "rashness" is also a more complicated concept here. In cases of psychological control, rashness might be viewed as breaking the emotional hold in a thoughtless or impulsive manner. However, there are times when acting rashly in cases of control would seem to be effective. A spouse in an abusive and controlling relationship may reach a point where "enough is enough" and suddenly break the relationship off. If time had been given to more reason and thought, the motivation to act may have been lost. But is this really *rashness*? Perhaps not. An act may be "spur of the moment" but what leads up to that moment is important. For the battered wife who suddenly leaves the relationship, the background can make the act rational. Courage may have to be "built up," as we say, before the act is performed. In that sense courage may require a moment of impetuousness within a larger context of understanding the situation.

Courage and the virtue of patience often need to balance each other in cases of psychological control. In any relationship like a marriage a tension exists between what to accept "as is" from your partner and what to try to change. For people trapped in a psychologically unhealthy relationship, the choice between patience and courage may be acute.[4] Patience is not cowardice though it might be an excuse for that. Patience is the virtue by which we continue to accept situations with either the expectation of a better future or the awareness of an overall good which justifies accepting negative elements. The parent of a child is patient because of a reasonable expectation of a change for the better down the road. A spouse in a marriage may be patient because, even though a particular pattern of behavior will probably not change, the overall good of the relationship justifies patience. But at some point patience can lead to exploitation. If the expectation of a better future is not reasonable based on the history of the relationship, then patience can be "false," and cowardice can begin to dominate. A parent whose adult child continues to exploit him after many broken promises of change is not acting on patience but on a fear of confronting the truth. Similarly, a woman who accepts a husband's violence or infidelities because of the larger good of the relationship has to look honestly at what the "good" entails. It may be fear that motivates acceptance of the negative behavior, not a positive good in the relationship. Counselors help clients all the time with such analyses. The ethical element enters when courage is required and the person must choose to act.

Lack of courage in relationships can easily facilitate harm. It happens innumerable times in marriages. A spouse may have an addiction or compulsion which is harming both partners and the relationship. Alcoholism is the most common example in our society but the problems could range from a gambling addiction to an addiction to Internet pornography. Patience has nothing to do with this—the problem may have been going on for a long time and is no minor issue to be balanced against a larger good. Your spouse's health is involved, the good of the children, the relationship. Self-deception may be easy for both parties but let's assume self-honesty here, at least by the spouse being manipulated by the addict. He or she fully acknowledges what is going on. The choice is clear and incredibly difficult. Act in a way to improve the situation. What that action should be will depend on the spouse and the situation but something must be done. Applying courage intelligently (with what Aristotle called practical wisdom) is not easy. Rashness often leads to pointless blow-ups or dead ends but cowardice continues a negative and harmful situation. A counselor may be critical in helping the spouse decide how to act most appropriately. But, in the end, courage is the number one virtue. Facilitating harm by allowing oneself to be manipulated is to make cowardice an ally of destruction.

MILGRAM REVISITED:
WHY "NO" IS SO HARD TO SAY FOR SO MANY PEOPLE

(The subject) begins the experiment calmly but becomes increasingly tense as the experiment proceeds. After administering the 180-volt shock, he pivots around in his chair and, shaking his head, addresses the experimenter in agitated tones:

SUBJECT: I can't stand it. I'm not going to kill that man in there. You hear him hollering?

EXPERIMENTER: As I told you before, the shocks may be painful, but—

SUBJECT: but he's hollering. He can't stand it. What's going to happen to him?

EXPERIMENTER (his voice is patient, matter-of-fact): The experiment requires that you continue, Teacher.

SUBJECT: Aaah, but, unh, I'm not going to get that man sick in there . . . know what I mean?

EXPERIMENTER: Whether the learner likes it or not, we must go on, through all the word pairs.

SUBJECT: I refuse to take the responsibility. He's in there hollering!

EXPERIMENTER: It's absolutely essential that you continue, Teacher.

SUBJECT (indicating the unused questions): There's too many left here; I mean, Geez, if he gets them wrong, there's too many of them left. I mean who's going to take the responsibility if anything happens to that gentleman?

EXPERIMENTER: I'm responsible for anything that happens to him. Continue, please.

SUBJECT: All right. . . . (At 315 volts)

LEARNER: I absolutely refuse to answer.

SUBJECT: You got to. You get a shock if you don't answer. (Experiment continues with learner refusing to answer, and, finally, failing even to grunt or groan. At 375 volts, the subject stands up.)

SUBJECT: I think something's happened to that fellow in there. I don't get no answer. He was hollering at less voltage. Can't you check in and see if he's all right, please?

EXPERIMENTER (with same detached calm): Not once we've started. Please continue, Teacher.

SUBJECT (sit down, sighs deeply): "Cool—day, shade, water, paint." Answer, please. Are you all right in there? Are you all right?

EXPERIMENTER: Please continue, Teacher. Continue, please. (Subject pushes lever.)

SUBJECT (swiveling around in his chair): Something's happened to that man in there. (swiveling back) Next one. "Low—dollar, necklace, moon, paint." (Turning around again) Something's happened to that man in there. You better check in on him, sir. He won't answer or nothing.

EXPERIMENTER: Continue. Go on, please.

SUBJECT: You accept all responsibility?

EXPERIMENTER: The responsibility is mine. Correct. Please go on. (Subject returns to his list, starts running through words as rapidly as he can read them, works through to 450 volts.)

Stanley Milgram, *Obedience to Authority*, 73–76.

In Milgram's shock experiment alluded to in chapter one, shocking other people to the point of pain and possibly death provided clear examples of self-justification. "I am a good person" and "I just shocked a screaming man" have to be reconciled somehow and, as noted, it is often done by downplaying the disturbing cognition ("the shocks aren't too bad") or building a bridge between the two cognitions ("the experimenter told me to do it"). In this section I want to explore in more detail why people in harmful or psychologically disturbing relationships fail to act to end those relationships or at least change them. Why do we continue to facilitate a harmful situation? What techniques do we use to maintain such relationships?

Milgram himself provided some answers in his analysis of his experiment.[5] With some modification and additions his reasons provide some insight into why courage is so difficult in harmful or dependency relationships. I want to examine three such reasons.

Politeness

This seemingly superficial character trait runs deep into the marrow of many people. It certainly is not a negative trait. But any virtue taken to an extreme becomes blind and destructive and politeness is no exception. Politeness at its best is consideration, tact and proper deference toward another individual. Without it misunderstanding and hostility can poison social interactions. Ideally, we are polite to each other because we respect each other's dignity or have a mutual relationship that needs to run smoothly. Nick may be polite to his teacher because he respects her. And he may be polite to an anonymous store employee because he is involved in a reciprocal relationship with that person in the roles of customer and clerk. Politeness allows the interchange to proceed smoothly. Politeness also comes into play when role differences involve differences in authority. Nick may be polite to his manager at work not only because he respects him as a person or because they work together as a team but because the role the manager fulfills deserves respect. Authority at its most genuine is authority *deserved* and politeness toward a manager or employer who has earned the authority of that position is as genuine a virtue as politeness between two friends.

The loss of politeness in a society signals a loss of empathy between people. For example, a simple phrase like "excuse me" to a stranger is a recognition of an unintended violation of the personal space of someone you may never see again. We say it because we recognize a mutual right to privacy and dignity among human beings and "excuse me" in this culture expresses that recognition. We are also aware at some level that, without politeness in such cases, hostility is a real possibility because we understand that the violation of others' personal space without their approval is a potential threat to them. Clearly the loss of such simple phrases like "excuse me" is more than just the loss of some superficial social etiquette. It indicates a loss of awareness of mutual dignity. We can no longer or are no longer willing to put ourselves in the stranger's situation and recognize that we share a common condition. As

Confucius saw more clearly than any other philosopher in history, the forms of social interaction reflect who we are as a people.[6] The loss of politeness can be a blow to the infrastructure of our society.

But politeness can become a vice. Respecting the dignity of others is a virtue but so is respecting your own dignity. Sometimes out of physical fear, sometimes out of fear of being alone or of being ostracized, and sometimes simply out of habit, people are polite to the extreme to those around them. They do not make distinctions about when, where or how to be polite. Parents can be so afraid of disciplining children or providing them with necessary limits that they are excessively "polite" to them. Or a child may be so fearful of independence that, as an adult, politeness to parents becomes a way of justifying not being assertive for oneself. Forms of politeness evolve in a healthy parent-child relationship. As a child matures, the parent must do a balancing act between politeness and respect on the one hand and the productive exercise of authority on the other. By the time the child is fully an adult, politeness should be much more between equals who respect each other. Throughout the parent-child relationship moments of courage arise, especially for parents, when politeness threatens to become a front for cowardice and fear.

Social pressure can lead to false forms of politeness. In Milgram's experiment many participants did not want to be rude to Milgram's assistant. Rather than risk hurting his feelings, they went on and continued to shock the learner. How often does this sort of experience occur in everyday life? How often does peer pressure force us into forms of politeness which are cover-ups for a fear to act or speak as we should? We do not want to be ostracized—it is a kind of social death. We fear our ego will disintegrate if left out of a group or forced to stand alone. We do not want to lose "friends." So we continue with the destructive habit, accept the verbal assaults, continue the kowtowing to irrational ideas or irrational authorities. Our life passes us by but we *are* polite about it. False politeness is an incredibly common example of lack of courage by human beings. If Milgram can get over half his participants to shock a screaming and pleading man to 450 volts because they did not want to be rude to the experimenter, what are the odds of us standing up for our integrity in a group of social acquaintances or fellow employees? We need to ask ourselves some questions. What *exactly* am I afraid of here? Which is genuinely worth more, my integrity in the situation or my continued smooth but superficial relationship to this group? The goal, as Aristotle would put it, is to act on politeness in the right place at the right time in the right way with the right people. The middle road here is a very narrow one. Loss of politeness turns a society into a place of chaos and distrust with irrational aggression always a step away. Too much politeness (or "false" politeness) becomes an easy excuse for cowardly behavior and nice words that can facilitate destructive behavior in marriages, friendships or any peer group. The middle road of genuine politeness reinforces one's own dignity as a human being and strengthens the fabric of society.

Hiding Behind a Role

In the shock experiment one way that the teachers avoided responsibility for shocking the learner was to focus on the process or technique. Some "teachers" ignored the screams and pleadings in the next room by focussing on getting the tasks done correctly such as saying the word pairs properly to the learner or giving the right verbal cues. This method of focusing on a process in order to avoid responsibility has much broader application than the shock experiment and is a significant way for people in harmful or destructive relationships to avoid difficult decisions.

The most common form of this phenomenon is hiding behind roles. In Milgram's experiment some of the "teachers" viewed the role given them by Milgram as a justification for not stopping the experiment. In everyday life this experience is quite common. Every marriage has numerous roles. While in the past these roles were quite clearly laid out by society, today they often have to be worked out couple by couple. Nevertheless, they are critical in the relationship. Who is expected to do what is central for any marriage to function. Some of these roles, such as who takes out the garbage, may be minor in themselves. But these smaller roles may be incorporated into larger more important roles such as who is in charge of the house, who is the main source of income or who is the primary care-giver for young children. Once roles are established, taking them seriously greatly helps to facilitate a happy marriage.

However, as with politeness, there is a "dark side" to role-taking. We can hide behind our roles so we do not have to make difficult decisions in a relationship. Unfortunately, a fairly common scenario is the following. A marriage is becoming difficult, perhaps because of some habit or addiction by one party, perhaps because of a communication or sexual problem, perhaps because of difficulties over money. In any case what happens is that each spouse begins to focus on the process, i.e., the role expectations he or she has as a way to avoid talking about or facing the problem. So, commonly, even with our more open and loosely–defined roles, the male will often focus on what "husbands" or "fathers" do—perhaps focus more than ever on being the bread-winner or handyman. Women nowadays may also dodge tough confrontations with spouses by focusing on work and earning power but many still will focus on the role of nurturer or care-giver. Obviously, as noted above, all of these roles, no matter who performs them, are critical in the success of a marriage. However, what happens is that the spouse starts putting the role *between* himself and the real problem. It becomes a type of armor worn by the person as a way to avoid courage. So, instead of dealing with the basic communication problem that exists, the husband goes off to his workshop. Or, instead of loving her spouse to the point of helping him deal with his alcohol addiction, the wife will push the role of "nurturer" to the forefront as a way of keeping things going smoothly and avoiding a difficult ordeal. Hiding behind the role in both cases facilitates the continuation of a problem. The communication problem is not resolved and the addiction becomes easier.

Hiding behind a role also occurs frequently in unhealthy situations of control. In the examples mentioned in the first part of this chapter, the parent who wants to continue to control an adult child will push the role of "parent" far beyond what is reasonable and then use that as a front for his or her actions. Likewise, the adult child who does not want to break away may continue to view the parent-child role relationship in the same way he or she did earlier in life. After all, I *am* still Mom and Dad's child and everyone knows that children should respect their parents' wishes. In some marriages one spouse may control the other in destructive ways behind the role of "protector" or "care-giver." Clearly, our society has a problem with people not taking their roles seriously. Far too many parents do not know or care what the role of "parent" involves. But the virtues people need in these cases are more often self-discipline, temperance, generosity and love. The vice we are discussing is much more a matter of a lack of psychological courage. Hiding behind a role to avoid independence or to avoid a problem in a relationship is at its core a lack of courage.

In the work environment hiding behind a role to avoid a difficult but important confrontation is quite common also. But an important difference from the home is that these roles are usually institutionalized and formal rewards (like salary) are attached to them. The hierarchy of a business necessarily involves control and manipulation but, as millions know, the line where that control is rational is often surpassed by managers or bosses. Responding to irrational control at work often ties moral courage into psychological courage. A woman experiencing sexual harassment by a manager at work stands up for her own psychological well-being by confronting the issue. This is psychological courage. But strong elements of moral courage exist in that a moral violation of her dignity as a person is occurring and the implication of confronting the abuse will probably have strong ripple effects on how other people are treated in her company or department. The formalized nature of roles in a business means that confrontation will be that much harder but also that much more important to other people who fill similar roles now and in the future.

The business environment provides an excellent example again of Aristotle's master virtue of *phronesis* or practical wisdom. Many people find themselves in the following situation. You have taken a job that supports yourself and perhaps your family and you generally enjoy the work. The money is important for a number of goals you or your family have set. A change in management occurs and a new manager comes aboard who turns out to have little respect for those under him. He goes well beyond the reasonable level of control and his verbal barbs, self-centered manipulation, and subtle threats start eating away not just at morale on the job but at your own psychological well-being. You leave work depressed or angry consistently. It feeds back into your family, you have trouble sleeping and your health is being affected. What should you do? Given the hierarchy in a business, confronting your manager or going over his head is dangerous. You could lose your job or the manager's behavior could actually get worse. Ideally, you can find some solution which saves the best of the situation by transferring to a different department or perhaps changing jobs to a different company in which your skills are as fully utilized. But what if those are not options? That is where "practical wisdom" is useful. Should you be courageous or put up with it, hoping for the best? Is courage for your own well-being of more value than the utilitarian good the money does for your family? You are not hiding behind the role in this case. You are attempting to be as brutally honest as possible and not be a coward. Certainly discussing the situation with your family, friends or a counselor will probably help a good deal. But in the end you must decide. Don't ignore it, deceive yourself about it or use phony excuses. If courage is required, act on it, being aware of possible consequences but with your head held high and dignity intact. If the utility of the job is simply too important, have a support group of some kind to help you work through it, perhaps on a daily basis. And, surely, take every possible means allowed by the business hierarchy to let the situation be known and the negative effects on the company brought to the awareness of those who can do something about it. All of these factors play into whether or not to confront the controller and how to do it. Psychological courage is embedded in a context of other goods and when and how to apply it is a matter of *phronesis*, the intellectual skill that helps you figure out the best road to take.

The Abuses of Duty

The emphasis on immediate gratification in this society produces habits in children in which performance of duties in life becomes difficult. This may start with not doing simple chores around the home but blossoms as an adult into an inability to follow through on duties and expectations. This is not a particularly mysterious connection. If a child has learned by habit to want things NOW, then putting off gratification until after the chores are done or the homework finished clashes with the expectation of gratification at the moment. One of the most difficult tasks of parenting today is to help children learn a sense of duty and responsibility in the face of a constant barrage of immediate pleasures. The phrase "a sense of duty" is an anachronism in a society where long-term projects are "boring" or results cannot be seen immediately.

But for many people the problem is not a lack of a sense of duty but an exaggerated one. An exaggerated sense of duty is certainly not taught by our society but is a common way for people in controlling or abusive relationships to justify their actions. Milgram's subjects often shifted responsibility to the experimenter, thus allowing them to do their duty. "Fred," the individual involved in the scene at the beginning of this section, twice asked Milgram's assistant who was responsible for the health of the screaming learner. When he was told by the experimenter, "I am responsible," Fred continued shocking the person. This phenomenon is common outside of psychology laboratories and applies to all three forms of courage. In a war a soldier told to perform what he knows is an atrocity may justify cowardice by claiming it was his duty and the responsibility was not his. With moral courage, instead of facing up to discrimination at work, an employee might claim it is none of his business. He has his own duties to perform and the problem is for those with more authority. In a case involving psychological courage in relationships, Joan may emphasize the duties she has which outweigh any responsibility to change an abusive situation. This is similar to hiding behind roles discussed above but with one difference. Here Joan is not just using her role as a "wife" to justify cowardice in her marriage; she is consciously shifting responsibility to the controlling partner ("He knows best") and focussing on a sense of duty to the person. Some people have an exaggerated sense of duty quite independent of whatever role they are in and this unrealistic sense of duty to the controlling person in a marriage, for example, becomes an excuse for not making the courageous choice.

An interesting moral phenomenon briefly noted by Milgram occurs frequently in such cases.[7] Normally, most people would consider the suffering they caused to an innocent person a motive for stopping. We are horrified when we see innocent people being hurt by others and most of us would feel strong guilt doing it ourselves. But in social situations in which control is an important function, many people shift their moral sense from suffering to the performance of duty. In other words, the sense of duty takes over our moral rudder and suffering takes second place. Now, there are times in which this shift may be justified. A nurse's actions which cause short-term suffering to a patient may be in the line of duty with the long-term good of the patient in mind. A parent's duty to her children may justify harming someone who would hurt them. But what kind of justification can be given for claiming that a duty to a stranger in a white lab coat justifies causing the potential death of an innocent person by electric shock? Enormous suffering and a small realistic sense of duty get completely twisted around by the person's fear of saying "no." The moral shift from suffering to duty is not justified by the conditions at hand and is motivated not by realism but by fear.

We face this same dilemma at times in relationships and in the business world. Theresa's spouse may be brutally hard on the children in a highly irrational way and her own self-esteem is under constant attack but, by emphasizing her duties to her husband and shifting all the responsibility to him, she can avoid a confrontation. Joe works at a company in which his boss is killing the morale and self-worth of those under him. Joe's own physical and psychological health, which had been excellent in the past, is now straining under the constant pressure of irrational attacks. He is fearful of confronting his boss or taking any action so he constantly shifts his moral compass to his sense of "duty" to the company. The suffering being forced upon him and other workers is ignored. As noted above, utilitarian factors may play a big role here, e.g., the money needed for his family, the likelihood of being fired and of finding a new job, etc. Nevertheless, part of the reason for failure to act may simply be fear of confronting the controller. As in the Milgram experiment, exaggerating a sense of duty keeps our self-image "safe" by running away from what needs to be done. Where awareness of suffering is normally critical to our moral sense, it now becomes submerged under an irrational sense of duty motivated by fear. Depth of character and a strong sense of self-confidence come from acting courageously when courage is called for.

IF ONLY THOSE OTHER PEOPLE HAD STRONGER CHARACTERS

Gessen was an artist monk. Before he would start a drawing or painting he always insisted upon being paid in advance, and his fees were high. He was known as the "Stingy Artist."

A geisha once gave him a commission for a painting. "How much can you pay?" inquired Gessen.

"Whatever you charge," replied the girl, "but I want you to do the work in front of me."

So on a certain day Gessen was called by the geisha. She was holding a feast for her patron.

Gessen with fine brush work did the painting. When it was completed he asked the highest sum of his time.

He received his pay. Then the geisha turned to her patron, saying: "All this artist wants is money. His paintings are fine but his mind is dirty; money has caused it to become muddy. Drawn by such a filthy mind, his work is not fit to exhibit. It is just about good enough for one of my petticoats."

Removing her skirt, she then asked Gessen to do another picture on the back of her petticoat.

"How much will you pay?" asked Gessen.

"Oh, any amount," answered the girl.

Gessen named a fancy price, painted the picture in the manner requested, and went away.

It was learned later that Gessen had these reasons for desiring money:

A ravaging famine often visited his province. The rich would not help the poor, so Gessen had a secret warehouse, unknown to anyone, which he kept filled with grain, prepared for these emergencies.

From his village to the National Shrine the road was in very poor condition and many travelers suffered while traversing it. He desired to build a better road.

His teacher had passed away without realizing his wish to build a temple, and Gessen wished to complete this temple for him.

After Gessen had accomplished his three wishes he threw away his brushes and artist's materials and, retiring to the mountains, never painted again.

> From "101 Zen Stories" in *Zen Flesh, Zen Bones*,
> edited by Paul Reps, Story #47.

Do you ever wonder why other people fail in circumstances that seem so obviously set up for victory? Certainly you and I would have acted more intelligently and done what was necessary. Or how about that boss of yours who comes in crabby almost every day? He must have some deep personality defect. It seems so obvious—why doesn't he do something about it? This tendency we have to judge other people by their inner disposition is called by social psychologists the fundamental attribution error. When the jargon is put aside, what that means is: You failed because you didn't try hard enough; I failed because I had a headache from staying up all night with my son. We explain the actions of others through internal causes. We tend to view the behavior of another person as the result of the "kind of person" he or she is while we are much less prone to judge ourselves that way.[8] This leads to critical misjudgments of other people and can have a profoundly negative effect on relationships, both personal and work-related. In this section I want to explore some of the factors that go into "attribution errors" and talk about ways that we can overcome what is basically the "easy way" of judging other people.

Why do we do this? Undoubtedly some of it ties closely into self-deception and self-justification issues described in chapter one. Mike deceives himself about his anger problem by convincing himself that other people are the cause. Or Lisa justifies her poor choice of a new car by claiming that it is a popular model and being seen in that model makes safety issues unimportant. Mike and Lisa do not let others off the hook so easily. Mike is quick to note that Mark's smoking problem is unfortunately the result of a weak will and Lisa views the shoddy quality of Sandy's new home as a statement about Sandy's poor aesthetic judgment. Many attribution errors concerning other people are tied to the need to justify our own behavior and make it look better by contrasting it with the inner failings of others. Courage in admitting mistakes would be the first step toward making attributions more accurately.

However, many reasons exist outside of self-deception or cognitive dissonance for why we attribute inner dispositions to others but not to ourselves. Imagine Matt is simply trying to understand the behavior of another person, e.g., Anne, the teacher in the night class he is taking. The first thing he would do would be to discount those actions that are either forced on the person or part of her accepted role. Thus, in understanding Anne, Matt would discount her taking the class roll or telling the class about school requirements since that is what all teachers do. Instead he would focus on actions that are freely chosen and out of the ordinary, i.e., actions that seem to be the unique choice of the individual. After the roll is taken, Anne gives a stern warning to the class that she means to take roll at each class session and anyone missing will clearly have his or her grade docked. Since she didn't have to do that, the action appears freely chosen and seems to say something about Anne. She has a definite tendency toward being a "tough" and controlling teacher. Since the action appears chosen, it seems to come from inside the person and therefore says something (not much, but something) about Anne's character or personality. Matt might add to himself at this point: Anne doesn't seem to have much respect for the fact that this class is all adults and we understand responsibility. The relationship is off to a rocky start.

Another factor in attribution is what psychologists Jones and Davis called "noncommon effects."[9] Matt begins to wonder, as often happens, why Anne is teaching this course, especially since it soon becomes apparent that Anne is not a great teacher. Consider two situations. In the first one, Anne's field is in great demand and highly lucrative. The school pays big money to get anybody at all to teach part-time in this area and Matt knows that Anne's firm looks highly on employees who work in the community on their own time. Why is she teaching this class? It could be any number of reasons—money, status, job enhancement. Not much is learned. But imagine Anne's field is not in great demand and the school pays adjunct lecturers peanuts. However, it is well-known that people who move up in Anne's firm must have a "name" in the community. Has Matt learned anything about Anne as a person? Since the only "noncommon effect" is the benefit her company puts on community involvement, he might well conclude (wrong or not) that Anne wants to move up in her firm by doing something extra in the community. A reasonable conclusion is that she is teaching this class for that effect. It is a way to get her name in the public eye. So Anne is not only tough; she is ambitious, a common trait in our capitalist society. Matt might add to himself: No wonder she is a poor teacher and doesn't respect us; she probably doesn't even want to be here. This class is a step on her way to the top of the corporate ladder.

But Anne is neither especially "tough" nor "ambitious." In fact she loves teaching. The college has been under academic pressure; too many graduates have been deemed unprepared by important members of the community who also are major contributors. In an effort to rectify this the President has sent around a confidential memo to all instructors to do everything possible to keep attendance and participation at a maximum in class. As the President said, "We must do everything we can to counter the image of being a second-rate school in which students can bluff their way through courses. Please cooperate in this regard." Anne, who is in her first year and who really wants to give teaching a shot as a career option, subsequently lays down a strict attendance policy with her class.

Anne also has a young family and her current salary in her job is minimal. If teaching doesn't work out in the long run, she is going to have to do *something* to give her children a decent chance in life. This part-time teaching job is one critical way to impress the company she is currently with. She actually is not interested in the status or power of a higher position. But teaching this course may affect future salary adjustments in the company and even small gains are money that can be saved for her family's future. Moreover, even though this college pays little to adjunct instructors, the amount she can earn teaching will make some difference. She is having trouble learning the ropes of how to be a good teacher but she is trying. Her love of her children is a powerful motivator.

So we have a basic misunderstanding not driven by vice on either side. The difference is that Matt judges Anne's actions by internal criteria, personality traits that we all understand such as "toughness" with a group of people you control and "ambition" to move up in a capitalistic system. Unaware of the other factors in Anne's life, he concludes that toughness and ambition are the driving internal causes of her actions. On the first point about toughness he is wrong because the actual cause is external—pressure on the instructors that he is unaware of. On the second point about ambition, he is wrong because lack of information leads to a wrong analysis of internal motivation—ambition vs. love of family. We all have Matt's tendencies: 1) to assume a simple internal cause for the actions of others while our own behavior is viewed to have multiple causes, most external; 2) to assume quickly that we know the internal cause in the other person that matches our experience ("ambition") without going out of our way to find out more information that is relevant. A great deal of misunderstanding, conflict and harm could be avoided if we did not act upon these attribution tendencies. Assume that the other person's behavior is motivated by as much complexity and external forces as yours and, when an internal cause is judged to be the source, make sure you have as much information as possible. Withholding judgments can be tough to do, especially if your peers are making judgments. A degree of psychological courage in admitting your own weakness is required here to avoid caving in to the quick judgment. Moral courage is also tied in because, after all, the judgment of Anne as a person, while not done for nefarious reasons, is grossly unjust compared to what her life is really like.

This phenomenon, in which the actions of others are judged quickly by internal characteristics which we assume are present while our own actions are excused by external causes, has been analyzed in several ways and is also called the "actor-observer" effect by social psychologists.[10] The actor-observer effect is an everyday occurrence for most people; it is hard to get through a day without making at least subtle judgments about the behavior of others. Someone is late for a meeting and our mind easily assumes lack of concern for other participants but when we are late, it is busy highways or family pressures. This is a simple difference but it can lead in some cases to justifying significant harm against others because of our automatic assumption that it is *their fault*. The will power or perseverance of those other people is just not strong enough and, therefore, they deserve what they get. Note—there is no question that inner motivation *is* important. But we need to be as accurate and just as possible in attributing personality characteristics to others.

Another related and common experience involving attributions is called the "self-serving bias" and has to do with how we judge positive and negative experiences that happen to us.[11] This also can create much unnecessary conflict and requires genuine courage at times to overcome. Imagine you and a group of three others are working on a joint project. In scenario one the project is a great success and your name is mentioned publicly as part of the team. To what would you attribute your success? Though you might give some verbal credit to the others, you would in your mind remember the hard work you put in and the skill it took for you to finish the project. You are deeply responsible for the project's success. In scenario two the project fails miserably and your name is also mentioned publicly. To what would you attribute your failure? The company set up the project poorly with insufficient funds and your co-workers never did pull their own weight. Your level of responsibility is minimal.

Certainly there is nothing surprising in the self-serving bias. While issues of cognitive dissonance and self-deception may play a big role at times, it is also quite natural to expect success in a project, especially a project you have worked hard on. If the project succeeds, simple cause and effect would indicate that your work produced the results you expected and hoped for. The irrational part of the self-serving bias is to overrate what you did and to make your own role more important than that of others when in fact it was not so. It also takes a good deal of courage to own up to our role in a failure. Quite aside from self-deception issues, it has to do with plain old human pride and a need to improve and protect self-image. Blocking excessive pride and taking a realistic look at the role you played requires the courage to accept yourself and often your role in a team project. Note that the opposite also occurs when it comes to success. There are many people who cannot accept success, who deliberately downplay their role to themselves and others. This tendency is less common than the positive bias but it also can be harmful. People can get in the habit of putting themselves down whenever they succeed, the result being a life with limited joy in the exercise of one's skills and abilities.

Finally, perhaps the most powerful form of attribution occurs with groups and it is here that moral and psychological courage and possibly physical courage take on a crucial role. We attribute desirable behaviors by members of our own in-groups to stable, internal causes like perseverance and a tendency to work hard. At the same time we attribute desirable behaviors by members of out-groups to luck or external causes. Prejudice and hatred are intermixed with such attributions. The need to increase our self-esteem by contrasting ourselves with others gets tied to identifiers like skin color, language or accent, and cultural rituals. Positive acts done by the other group are considered transient or reflective of traits less significant in the big scheme of life. Negative acts done by the other group reflect stable, internal traits that are central to defining "human" behavior. Likewise, positive acts by our group reflect our inherent superior qualities while negative acts are transient, the product of deviant individuals or reflective of traits that aren't very important anyway. Why we do this is still subject to much debate but certainly one simple reason is that my self-image is not enhanced if my social group is not perceived as superior in some way. Thus my social group must have strong positive inherent qualities. Since we all are members of social groups and we want to feel positive about who we are, we naturally identify and exaggerate those tendencies which support our self-image. While this identification may be harmless in a game between two high school basketball teams, it can be genocidal when applied to ethnic groups and combined with dissonance reduction and self-deception.

Psychological and moral courage are monumental here. How? Psychological courage: 1) admitting your own weaknesses in the face of in-group pressure, 2) being as objective as possible in attributions about your group's characteristics despite blows to your own self-image in the process, 3) being as objective as possible in attributions about the other group's characteristics while putting your own ego needs on hold. Moral courage: 1) standing up for justice and rights between people despite strong tendencies to attribute characteristics based on identifying markers like skin color or accent, 2) facing down your own group's unjust attributions and saying so, 3) having the moral integrity to face possible ostracism and social rejection. Obviously, as shown in history, physical courage in facing pain and suffering may also be involved. If learning to live together on an increasingly small planet is *the* human project right now, then courage is the central virtue for each of us in the struggle for just and fair attributions toward each other.

LET THE OTHER PERSON TAKE CARE OF IT

Perhaps someone may say 'But surely, Socrates, after you have left us you can spend the rest of your life in quietly minding your own business.' This is the hardest thing of all to make some of you understand. If I say that this would be disobedience to God, and that is why I cannot 'mind my own business', you will not believe me—you'll think I'm pulling your leg. If on the other hand I tell you that to let no day pass without discussing goodness and all the other subjects about which you hear me talking and examining both myself and others is really the very best thing that a man can do, and that life without this sort of examination is not worth living, you will be even less inclined to believe me . . . For my own part I bear no grudge at all against those who condemned me and accused me, although it was not with this kind intention that they did so, but because they thought that they were hurting me; and that is culpable of them. However, I ask them to grant me one favour. When my sons grow up, gentlemen, if you think that they are putting money or anything else before goodness, take your revenge by plaguing them as I plagued you; and if they fancy themselves for no reason, you must scold them just as I scolded you, for neglecting the important things and thinking that they are good for something when they are good for nothing. If you do this, I shall have had justice at your hands, both I myself and my children.

Well, now it is time to be off, I to die and you to live; but which of us has the happier prospect is unknown to anyone but God.

Plato, *The Apology* in *The Last Days of Socrates*,
translated by Hugh Tredennick and Harold Tarrant, 63, 67.

Why does the presence of other people so often put a damper on our moral conscience? How can certain individuals like Socrates and Gandhi act against the pressures of "group think?" Most of us are prone to spread out responsibility to those we are with. Acting for what we know is best can get diffused by the very presence of other people. If you are alone and hear someone who desperately needs help, odds are high that you will help. But if you are with a group of five strangers who do not share a common goal, odds are low that you will help. Why this peculiar difference? This situation seems to be related to the Milgram experiment again but there are crucial differences. In this case nobody is ordering you to do anything. No authority figure is around to check up on you. No—this is a different type of group dynamic in which the relationship between a group of people has something to do with preventing or hindering a required action. A great deal of harm has occurred because people have not had the courage to step out of a group to perform a necessary action. Like Socrates, people in history we admire as moral heroes have had that courage.

This diffusion of responsibility is called by psychologists the "bystander effect." Classic cases often make the popular press. Kitty Genovese was killed while dozens of people sat in their apartments and watched. But the bystander effect is far more pervasive than cases that make headlines. What the evidence in psychology indicates is that this effect is not the result of some great cultural shift toward apathy or lack of caring in our society. When we are alone as individuals in cases where our assistance is needed, the vast majority of us act in a caring and empathetic way. The bystander effect is a human phenomenon that has to do not with some general moral decline but with the way we perceive our sense of responsibility when with a group of people. The result of this can be significant because *no one* ends up taking responsibility. Understanding our own motivation is a big step toward overcoming the bystander effect but clear elements of courage also are present. Latane' and Darley, two of the pioneer researchers in this area, have noted five decisions or steps in the bystander effect that lead to helping or not helping someone in need.[12] I want to look at these steps from the standpoint of courage. As an example, let's imagine Jennifer waiting for a bus with a group of other people when a man across the street cries out, stumbles and falls.

Attending to the Emergency

The first stage is whether Jennifer notices this at all. Whether an event is noticed might be sheer luck at times but often it also has to do with certain habits people get into, a certain level of attentiveness to people's needs. In

a fascinating experiment on this issue, Darley and Batson tested seminarians who were on their way to give a talk on the Good Samaritan parable.[13]
Some of them were told they were ahead of schedule, others that they were
right on schedule and a third group was told that they were going to be late.
On the way to the talk the experimenter set up a man who was coughing
and groaning and slumped in a doorway. Of those who were told they were
ahead of schedule, 63% stopped to help, of those who were told they
were right on schedule, 45% stopped to help, and, of those who were told
they were late, only 10% stopped to help. These were seminarians on their
way to give a talk about the Good Samaritan, some of whom stepped right
over the victim! What is equally interesting is the 10% who did stop despite the fact that they would be late for an important engagement. Empathy and awareness of others' needs seem to predispose people to help.
Courage is not so much an issue here as the need to develop habits of
empathy.

Perceiving that an Emergency Exists

If Jennifer does notice the man falling, she has to perceive it as an emergency.
Here courage starts to play a role. How? An unusual situation calls for more
information. The vast majority of people will not act until the evidence is
clear because they do not want to look stupid and be embarrassed. Well, how
do you get more information? It means going out of your way to find out. But
going out of your way to find out can be embarrassing. What if the guy across
the street looks young and healthy otherwise? Maybe he just slipped. What if
he has a bottle in his hand? What if Jennifer could not see what happened
clearly? What is going on here? When more than one person is involved in an
ambiguous but decisive situation, we tend to rely on each other to interpret
what is happening. So, if the people next to Jennifer do nothing, Jennifer will
have a much stronger tendency to interpret the event as not requiring her attention. This is called "pluralistic ignorance" and such "ignorance" is common as an excuse for inaction. In a situation of potential emergency, relying
on the responses of others in the group for information gives up far too much
of your own decision–making to others. What harm can be done by checking
when it is possible that somebody's life is at stake? The fear to be overcome
is embarrassment and a potential blow to one's self-image if it turns out to be
a misunderstanding. Without the courage to overcome some very trivial
fears—possible embarrassment before some people she does not even
know—Jennifer may never find out and a man may die. Overcoming "pluralistic ignorance" is the first step in psychological courage in beating the bystander effect.

Determining Responsibility to Help

Jennifer crosses the street and finds out the man seems to be having a seizure. Many thoughts go through her head. "There are a lot of people around here now. Some might be a lot better trained than me. Who am I to help this man?" "I might look like a real fool here." "If I do something and it's wrong, the man might die." "He might be an alcoholic or drug addict and he brought it on himself." "A lot of seizures are temporary and people get over them quickly. Trying to do something might make things worse." "If I am late for work again, my boss may fire me." Unless a person were especially trained, these types of thoughts would be common. Some of them are in the best interests of the person. "If I do something and it is wrong, the man might die." Some of them diffuse responsibility to the group. "Who am I to help this man?" Some of them are quite self-centered. "I might look like a fool." Some of them blame the victim. "He might be a drug addict and he brought it on himself." How does a person sort these out?

Courage is required to overcome, first, the self-centered excuses. Without overcoming the fear of looking foolish or stupid, nothing gets done. Jennifer must make a *choice* that vanity is worth less than the fact of suffering and possible death in front of her. Courage is also required to overcome, second, the diffusion excuses and the tendency to blame the victim. Unless Jennifer hears from someone else that he or she is especially trained, it is unlikely that, in a random group of people, someone knows a great deal more than she does. "Others" are not going to come riding over the hill like the cavalry. The diffusion excuses are natural but cowardly ways to avoid acting in an unknown precarious situation. The same is true for excuses that blame the victim. Yes, people are responsible for their lives. But what does a stranger know of someone else's life style and character? Even if the person had a bottle in his hand, what does that tell Jennifer about the other person's life? His goals, fears, loved ones, current situation? It is so incredibly easy to make some very fast generalizations about the victim as a way to avoid acting in the situation. The altruistic thoughts are a different story because Jennifer is quite right about being afraid of doing the wrong thing and creating more harm. Sorting out the situation seems to work like this: Have the psychological courage to overcome the self-centered, victim-blaming and diffusion excuses. Then, as well as you can, focus on the appropriate response for the person *without* those added fears and mind-traps as a burden.

Knowing What to Do and Deciding to Help

So Jennifer decides to help. But what should she do? Lack of knowledge may be the final barrier. Courage is needed to avoid using lack of knowledge as a final excuse to do nothing. With this last excuse behind her she now needs to have a clear head about how best to help. That may mean calling the paramedics immediately, knocking on someone's door or, if it honestly looks like she can do something herself, doing it. Each situation will be different. But the key point is that Jennifer is now free from phony excuses and irrational fears and can make choices that fit the situation. Those choices always involve risk but in some situations in life failure to act is itself an action. She has overcome any problems with her self-image or what people will think. She has overcome the easy out that "others" will take care of it and some vague excuse that the seizure is the victim's fault and not her responsibility. And she has overcome the easy retreat into ignorance about what to do as an excuse for doing nothing. She makes choices and takes responsibility. Psychological courage has given Jennifer a quantum leap in personal integrity. Socrates would be proud.

NOTES

1. Carolyn Swift, "Surviving: Women's Strength through Connection" in *Abuse and Victimization across the Life Span*, ed. M. Straus (Baltimore: Johns Hopkins University Press, 1988), 153–69. See also chapter 5 of Carol Gilligan, *In A Different Voice: Psychological Theory and Women's' Development* (Cambridge: Harvard University Press, 1982).

2. Aaron Beck, Arthur Freeman, and Associates, *Cognitive Therapy of Personality Disorders* (New York: The Guilford Press, 1990), 289–91.

3. Gerald Davison and John Neale, *Abnormal Psychology*, revised 6th edition (New York: John Wiley & Sons, 1996), 355–56.

4. Eamonn Callan, "Patience and Courage," *Philosophy*, 68, (1993): 523–39.

5. Stanley Milgram, *Obedience to Authority* (New York: Harper & Row, 1974), 7–12.

6. *The Essential Confucius*, trans. Thomas Cleary (San Francisco: Harper San Francisco, 1992), 1–11.

7. Milgram, *Obedience*, 8.

8. Robert Baron and Donn Byrne, *Social Psychology: Understanding Human Interaction* (Boston: Allyn and Bacon, 1994), 63–64.

9. Edward Jones and Keith Davis, "From Acts to Disposition: The Attribution Process in Person Perception" in *Advances in Experimental Social Psychology*, ed. L. Berkowitz (New York: Academic Press, 1965), Vol. 2, 219–66.

10. Edward Jones and Richard Nisbett, *The Actor and the Observer: Divergent Perceptions of the Causes of Behavior* (Morristown, New Jersey: General Learning Press, 1971).

11. Baron and Byrne, *Social Psychology*, 65–66.

12. Bibb Latané and John Darley, *The Unresponsive Bystander: Why Doesn't He Help?* (New York: Appleton-Century-Crofts, 1970.)

13. John Darley and Charles Batson, "From Jerusalem to Jericho: A Study of Situational and Dispositional Variables in Helping Behavior," *Journal of Personality and Social Psychology* 27 (1973): 100–8.

Chapter Four

The Rewards of Courage

No one questions the rewards of physical courage. Aristotle praises the "citizen-soldiers" who defended Athens. Those who fought in the Second World War protected freedoms you and I can now take for granted—freedom of assembly, speech, religion, press. Likewise, the value of moral courage is self-evident, from a courageous stand against polluting a river to the beautiful prose of King's "Letter from the Birmingham City Jail." This chapter specifically addresses the rewards of psychological courage. These rewards include benefits to ourselves, to society, and to our personal relationships ranging from friendships to marriage. I want to begin with the rewards of courage in maintaining and deepening intimate relationships.

THE REWARDS OF A LOVING RELATIONSHIP

To have faith (in another person) requires courage, the ability to take a risk, the readiness even to accept pain and disappointment. Whoever insists on safety and security as primary conditions of life cannot have faith; whoever shuts himself off in a system of defense, where distance and possession are his means of security, makes himself a prisoner. To be loved, and to love, need courage, the courage to judge certain values as of ultimate concern—and to take the jump and stake everything on these values. . . .

The practice of faith and courage begins with the small details of daily life. The first step is to notice where and when one loses faith, to look through the rationalizations which are used to cover up this loss of faith, to recognize where one acts in a cowardly way, and again how one rationalizes it. To recognize how every betrayal of faith weakens one, and how increased weakness leads to new betrayal, and so on, in a vicious circle. Then one will also recognize that while one is consciously afraid of not being loved, the real, though usually unconscious fear is that of loving. To love means to commit oneself without guarantee, to give oneself completely in the hope that our love will produce love in the loved person. Love is an act of faith, and whoever is of little faith is also of little love.

Erich Fromm, *The Art of Loving*, 106–7.

Awareness

The previous chapter discussed several examples in which a decision involving courage had to be made in the midst of social interaction. Such decision points are important in relationships like a marriage. One such point involves awareness. Studies indicate a greater potential for satisfying marriages when both partners are aware of the emotional flow of the ongoing relationship and communicate about that flow.[1] Put another way, the partners "track" the relationship. The current state of the relationship is never far from their minds. Why does this involve courage? Three reasons. First, becoming aware and staying aware of a relationship means confronting your own thoughts and actions honestly. Self-covering make accurate tracking impossible. Jason does not want to admit his need to control his mate so everything he "reads" from the relationship gets filtered through that need. Accurate awareness of his own emotional state is skewed by anxiety over control and thus his mate's words and actions are rarely looked at from her standpoint. Without courage to face his own anxiety, the tracking of the emotional flow in the relationship is rarely accurate.

Second, psychological courage is required to track the words and actions of one's mate accurately. This is a challenge independent of any anxiety about self. Tracy has been quite good at understanding the emotional flow in her marriage. After 15 years she understands her husband well. Unfortunately, her husband is changing and Tracy's stubborn certainty about her previous "tracking record" prevents her from being aware of those changes. The way she understands her husband emotionally is set in a rut. The result is an increasing distance between herself and her husband, a distance she may not even be aware is occurring. Accurate tracking of a relationship is impossible if we do not destroy the "superstructure" mentioned in chapter two. Unlike Jason, Tracy's inability to read her husband is not a function of her own obsessive anxieties. It is a function of images or "emotion thoughts" which she did not change over time. Being able to track a relationship accurately and being emotionally responsive in a relationship means being willing when necessary to drop out of our "comfort zone" with the image we have of our mate. That takes courage.

Third, psychological courage is important for awareness because the *attitude* a person has when he or she tracks the relationship is essential. Michael is very much aware of the emotional issues involved with his wife. The relationship is never far from his mind. But Michael's attitude toward the relationship has become increasingly negative. He tracks the relationship with Rachael so that he can find more ammunition to use against her. This is (and Michael probably knows it) a one-way road to the end of the relationship. He once remembered a counselor saying: If a person is going to be in a relationship, he or she should have the guts to either work at making it a positive experience or get out of it. But Michael has such pent-up resentment that those words ring hollow. Meanwhile, the hostile relationship continues on, taking away the precious moments of a lifetime. The courage here for Michael is to change his fundamental attitude toward the relationship which might be extremely hard to do. Whatever it is that is bothering him, *get to it*, deal with it. If he doesn't have the ability or desire to do that, at least have the courage to stop hurting his partner and, if necessary, end the relationship. So tracking with a positive and loving attitude is a real asset to a successful marriage and courage may play a role at several places along the way.

Dealing with Differences

Tracking a relationship positively means being aware of our partner's differences from our own emotional and intellectual expectations and being open to improving life together. But what do we do then? Ellen's husband has taken a new job and is completely dedicated to it. He spends far more time at work than he used to do and his time with Ellen and the children has been cut back severely. He gets home tired and, even on his days off, he seems distracted by issues from work. Ellen is aware of the family's emotional needs and is worried both for the children's relationship with their father and for her relationship with her husband. When she thinks about it, she has several options (none of which are easy): 1) Communicate and discuss the change in her husband's life and try to work with him on a solution. Then decide whether to accept the result; 2) If communication or compromise fails, emotionally accept the changes in her husband as much as possible with a positive attitude and do her best for all involved; 3) If communication or compromise fails, emotionally reject the changes in her husband but stay in the relationship, hoping for the best with the children's interest in mind; 4) If communication or compromise fails, reject the changes in her husband and work toward ending the relationship. This scenario is common in one degree or another in many marriages and the options all involve risk and loss.

In the best of all possible worlds, the first option would work out smoothly. Ellen and her husband sit down, openly discuss the issue, and reach a compromise because each loves the other and the children. In this first scenario her attempt to communicate would be successful and her husband would see what is happening and make appropriate changes in his career goals. In order for this to occur, it takes genuine psychological courage for Ellen to be honest about her own fears without self-deception ("Oh, there is no change in our relationship.") and then to confront a man whom she loves with a disturbing situation, a confrontation that could in itself rupture the relationship. She needs the courage to take the risk of communication, to be assertive when necessary, and to be flexible in her own mind about possible arrangements. If her husband is tracking the relationship at all with a positive and caring attitude, the future looks much more promising than the past. If her husband is less open to change, she will have to make difficult, heart-wrenching decisions about how much to accept of the situation.

What if her spouse is not open to change at all? What if he insists he still loves her and the family but this job is a once-in-a-lifetime opportunity and he cannot change his priorities? Or what if he simply refuses to communicate about it? Ellen then has options reflected in the other choices above. She recognizes that a number of other values come into play and her response is important for maintaining these values. One option is to basically surrender to the situation with a positive attitude and make the best out of it for herself and the children. This is *neither* cowardice nor self-deception if 1) she has tried to communicate and failed (and tried as many times as realism dictates), 2) she is fully aware of her own response and is not lying to herself either about her own feelings or the situation in the marriage, 3) she is honest about the other values involved in her decision (such as the children). The Stoics are again relevant here. There are times when the best we can do is control our own attitude so why not choose our life positively? It is entirely possible that breaking up the relationship would produce far greater harm all-around, although Ellen has to be very careful not to exaggerate the potential harm as a way to avoid making decisions or to hide behind a fear of being assertive. If she honestly decides that the family should stay intact, then it takes real courage to sacrifice some goals, modify plans, and rearrange her life to make it a positive experience. This is a form of psychological courage present in many marriages. And, in an unjust sexist society, women have most often had to make the choice. It is far too easy for outsiders to judge a relationship and say things like "why don't they just split up" or "why doesn't she leave him." Unless one is in that relationship, a person cannot completely understand the multiple values (emotional, family, issues of meaning in life) that can exist in a particular marriage or partnership. We need to realize and be much more sympathetic with the fact that a significant difference between partners in a marriage does not necessarily mean ill will and does not prevent other important values from being realized.

Ellen, and millions of people like her, can be open and caring people who have to make an honest and very difficult decision.

The third option is also quite common but tragic. *Rejecting* her spouse emotionally but continuing to put up with it is a traumatic, energy-draining and depressing way to live. It is continuing a marriage with alienation between the two partners. Nevertheless, that also may be the only choice at times, given some very difficult conditions. Since Ellen does ultimately have control over her own inner attitude, living with disdain and possibly hatred toward her spouse seems like a last resort. For the sake of her own sanity, going back to the previous option, if at all possible, seems like a better way to live. Sometimes, perhaps often, choosing a positive attitude in full awareness of the situation for the sake of oneself and other family members may be a truly courageous act.

But all too often such acceptance can lead to exploitation and a positive emotional choice becomes unbearably hard. And all too often the other values in a relationship, when honestly weighed, do *not* justify acceptance of a life of loneliness or noncommunication. (This "weighing" is best done not alone but with a trusted friend or counselor). Then yet another form of psychological courage is needed—the courage to break up a bond that may have deep emotional ties. Since an enormous amount has been written about divorce, suffice it to say here that, after communication in all possible forms has failed, if Ellen, in all honesty and empathy, decides that she cannot accept the changes in her husband and that other values genuinely would suffer by maintaining the marriage, her courage in choosing to opt for a brighter future for herself and the children should be praised, not condemned. This is not a decision made for self-centered or hedonistic reasons of an easier lifestyle nor is it a decision made with self-deception or some phony rationale. Those are cowardly reasons for breaking a relationship. It is a decision made in the full light of day, so to speak, with full awareness of options and for the best for all concerned, including her own life and that of other family members. If marriage is to mean anything, it should never be "easy." It *should* take real courage to either maintain a relationship or to end one and that is a decision that will almost certainly have to be made more times than on your wedding day. Shame, embarrassment or guilt should never result from an honest, thoughtful and courageous decision.

Overcoming Boredom

Marriages often face the opposite challenge of dealing with differences. Boredom and routine can kill relationships, whether they be marriages or simply friendships.[2] Courage would not seem to be a relevant virtue when it comes to overcoming boredom. What fear is there to face? At least one—the fear of breaking routine. Trying something new is a common, garden-variety fear for most of us. But, in an intimate relationship, a source of much more intense fear is breaking the emotional routine. After twenty years of marriage Robert and Maria know each other very well indeed. They can anticipate each other's actions, thoughts and emotions. They are, to put it best, not unhappy in their relationship. However, the repetition and the lack of new stimulation is starting to wear away at them. Since both are good trackers of the relationship's emotional state, they decide to try some changes. Some are relatively painless and help a little—they dine out more often and try different restaurants. They have varied their sex life though, after twenty years, the pleasure of sexual variety is not what it was in the first few years of marriage. Robert and Maria are both beginning to understand why the term "mid-life crisis" is more than just a cliche and the thought of another sexual partner brings to life feelings that seem to have gone dormant. But they do not want to destroy their relationship. Some deeper lifestyle changes may bring a sense of challenge back to them personally and deepen their love for each other. But it's a risky move; it might destroy what they currently have.

Consider, for example, the option of both of them returning to school part-time as a way to challenge their minds and stimulate the sharing of new experiences. Unlike finding a new restaurant in town, returning to school opens up uncharted thought patterns. What started out as a joint history course might turn into more history courses for Maria while Robert finds he hates history. In fact, she's got a crazy idea about going to graduate school in history while he now thinks the whole idea of returning to school was a waste of time. It is as if they were returning to their "pre-marriage" days and finding new life patterns to explore. This is exactly the solution for boredom but it can also bring challenges to the relationship that can be extremely painful. If Maria goes to graduate school, what happens to the life they've grown accustomed to for the last twenty years? What started out simply as a way to bring new stimulation to their marriage now becomes a potential threat to what was before a stable but routine relationship.

Many couples in this situation know ahead of time that the real cures for boredom are going to challenge them emotionally and lead to a potential threat to the relationship. That is where courage comes into the picture. Stability and routine are not bad in themselves; in many situations they are clearly positive and important. But routine can become boredom and boredom can kill a relationship and it is at this point that an individual or couple must choose to face or not face the fear that new challenges can bring. Some couples will choose long-term relatively unchanging routines—boredom is less of an issue, perhaps because both partners like routines or because the relationship is rich in ways beyond routine. Other couples need to find ways to renew their relationship regularly and some of those options for renewal and stimulation may involve overcoming fears of the unknown.

The Courage to Love Actively

In chapter one courage and compassion were linked because of the courage it takes to overcome our own narcissistic fears and open up to the needs of another person. In this section I want to explore in more detail the relationship of courage to caring about someone else. Perhaps the most original and astute analysis of caring for an intimate other was by the psychologist Erich Fromm in his classic little book, *The Art of Loving*.[3] In order to flesh out specifically how courage is involved in loving another person, I want to utilize three of Fromm's major points about love and expand on them in terms related to psychological courage.

Fromm claims that people are confused about the meaning of the term "love" and identifies three main reasons why. The first is the confusion between being loved and loving.[4] Most people are concerned about being *lovable*; they are not nearly as concerned about how to love and care about another person. This is natural in many ways, e.g., watch other creatures try to look good for a potential mate. However, as Fromm notes, being lovable has become a social obsession and people have become deeply confused about what "love" means. People spend billions in Western society trying to make themselves look or appear more acceptable and lovable. The result is a type of cultural narcissism with deep roots in our economic and social systems. Ads continually hit us with the idea that looking good to others is what a relationship is all about. Teenagers starve themselves at least partly due to a cultural milieu that says a person is not acceptable if he or she does not look a certain way. The diet and cosmetic industries are booming. But a person will have to look long and hard in popular culture for any concern about how to actually care for others. Community service ads, sex manuals for couples, sermons in churches—all have some valuable ideas for how to love actively. But frequently there is an ulterior motive—publicity, money, or a ticket to an afterlife. Fromm's argument is that the art of loving is fulfilling in itself and the definition of love as being "lovable" is a tragic distortion of an expansive, creative act turned into a self-centered and narcissistic one.

But what's wrong with wanting to look good to others? It is a sign of mental health to care about oneself and to have a positive self-image around other people and, if you do love someone, surely wanting to look good to that person is a sign of love. But I think most people who reflect at all on their lives know there is a difference between narcissistic vanity and wanting to present a positive social image, between looking good as a way to be lovable and looking good because you care about the other person. The same simple act, e.g., fixing one's hair or dressing well, can have very different motives. For Tim good grooming means people may pay more attention to him (which he craves) and he can experience yet another sexual conquest. For Paul good grooming means that the person he loves can be proud to be with him. A constantly fluctuating line exists because "me-focus" and "other-focus" in life. Fromm's point is that the more a person focuses on being lovable, the more he or she will lose the genuine joy of being able to care about others.

What does this have to do with courage? A great deal. Consider the following three examples. Anita is anorexic and convinced that she is "fat" while actually starving herself to death. Her desire to be lovable and acceptable is killing her. We now know there is a large physiological and chemical component to this disorder. Nevertheless, it takes enormous psychological courage for Anita to admit she has a problem and then to overcome the overwhelming psychological and social pressures in order to accept herself. Only when she is able to do that will she be able to know the joys of sharing herself with others. Anita must learn to "love" herself, not in the narcissistic sense but as a person with dignity and respect capable of acting positively and creatively with others.

Jake has spent almost all his entire life trying to impress others. Good-looking as a child, he came to have his self-image depend on the superficial impressions of him by other people. He learned by buying the best clothes, eating at the best restaurants, being seen with the "right" people, and saying the "right" things that people would like him and be impressed. You would not want to have a personal relationship with Jake. He has almost no ability to care genuinely about the needs of another person; everything he does is self-centered and this gets reinforced by society constantly telling him he looks good. Jake rarely thinks about his inner life beyond what the next person will think of him. Honest emotional reactions are rare and self-knowledge of his emotions is close to nonexistent. The only mistakes he admits are wearing the wrong suits. It is not going to happen that one day out of the blue Jake will simply say: Gosh, I think I'll become a sensitive, caring person and by magic he will effortlessly change his personality. If such a change were to occur, perhaps spurred on by broken relationships or an awareness of death or the superficiality of his life, it will take considerable courage for Jake to change. Giving up his self-image as "lovable" in order to learn how to love actively will mean facing some deep-seated fears and making some life-changing decisions.

Unlike Jake, Allen never got admired for his physical looks. In fact, he had quite the opposite experience as a child; he knew first hand the hatred of bullies and the put-downs of other children for not being "cool." So Allen took a different route. He became obsessed with reacting against his old self-image and, starting with adolescence, decided he would force other people to pay attention to him by becoming lovable and acceptable to society. Allen and Jake may visit the same stores, Jake to reinforce the image society has always had of him, Allen to feed the obsessive need to look good in opposition to what society thinks. Allen needs yet another variant of psychological courage—accepting himself without obsessive anxiety and facing down what society thinks while maintaining personal dignity and respect.

So we have many ways to spend our lives trying to be "lovable" to the point where it blocks or deters us from genuine caring. If Fromm is right, and I believe he is, the most joyous, transcendent moments in life are when our self gets *out of the way* and we can genuinely care about a person, project or task greater than ourselves. It takes courage to overcome the narcissistic shell of our self and open up to others.

Fromm's second major point is that people confuse the *object* of love with the *faculty* of loving.[5] Put another way, people often think that if the right person comes along, love will be easy. This is fed, Fromm claims, by ideas of romantic love (the "soul-mate" concept today) and by our capitalist system which always emphasizes getting a good bargain, the right object. So we think of the love object as being much more important than the process of how to love. This point about finding the right object of love dovetails with the previous one in that the object very often is found desirable because he or she makes *me* look good. But Fromm's point here has independent validity.

Overcoming the "love object" mentality would appear to take less psychological courage than overcoming the "need to be lovable" mentality. The issue is less about a fear to love and open up and more about a confusion about how to do that. The "love object" mentality awaits the right object but the person is not a coward about caring. However, Fromm's point is that the person who has practiced the art of loving will realize that the object of love is less critical than most people think. The object of your love *is* important—wisdom in selecting someone or something to care for is a critical component of how joyful or fulfilling love will be. However, the object of love cannot be a *substitute* for the practice of loving and that is where the problem lies. A wise choice is one thing; the "perfect" choice is something else. The key is to be unafraid of loving actively yet making wise choices in the process. What can happen is that, perhaps out of fear of actively caring, a person will focus on the perfect object of potential love as an excuse for not facing her own fears. When that happens, courage is central in dropping excuses ("I haven't found the right person") and living an open, actively caring life. The perfect object not found can become a cover for a fear of opening up to another person or taking the risk of a relationship. Without overcoming that fear, the perfect object of love will likely never appear or, if a person "settles" for less, resentment or a sense of "failed love" may permeate the relationship. If love is viewed as a faculty, a process one can practice and learn, then the object can be more variable and one can genuinely care for a wider range of people. Since the object of love does not define success, happiness lies as much in the process of loving as in the object of that love.

Fromm's third major point about love has much to do with courage—the confusion between infatuation and genuine love or between "falling in love" and "standing in love."[6] When the intense emotion fades, then comes the challenge of making a relationship work. Courage here has to do with facing shifting perceptions about the other person, a fear of losing the "high" of infatuation, and a fear of failure in the relationship. When your partner has flaws that you never noticed before, how will you handle it? How will you respond when the intense feeling of oneness is no longer a common one and two *individuals* must live together? What should you do when the loss of infatuation threatens the relationship itself, when a sense of emptiness starts to enter what was before the most emotionally intense time in your life? Courage is the number one virtue here—courage to face your partner honestly, courage to face your own set-in-stone perception of what a relationship is about, courage to communicate (often very difficult when infatuation goes), and courage to push yourself past the emptiness and fear of failure to try to build a relationship with somebody you claim you are committed to. The loss of infatuation is a situation rife with disappointment and fear.

Psychologists have suggested several reasons why relationships tend to sour or become more difficult after infatuation ceases.[7] Two of those are especially worth noting. The nature of close relationships is such that greater opportunity exists to discover a partner's faults. Once partners begin to feel confident with each other, they let down their guard, so to speak. Typically, even in the modern world of common premarital relations, people will attempt to consistently put their best self forward when they are with someone they feel passionate about. The traditional dating situation is a classic example. But after two people have committed to each other and infatuation fades, other aspects of their personalities may come forward—not necessarily harmful or destructive aspects but less than ideal. And being together allows each partner a maximum opportunity to observe those. Psychological courage is dealing with the fear of giving up our ideal perception of the person we were infatuated with and facing the reality of the other. Some people refuse to do this and live in a form of fantasy world as a relationship goes on. Others do change their perception of their mate but feel then that life has cheated them or that they have to settle for second best. But courage allows partners to deal with each other as real people without illusions and start to build a solid relationship from there.

A second factor behind the disillusionment that can occur after infatuation fades is lack of motivation. When we are with a social group that is not intimate, we often put a great deal of effort into listening and being polite. This can take a high level of awareness and marshalling of emotional resources. When we get back to an intimate setting and especially after the initial passion of infatuation has faded, we tend to relax. The motivation to listen carefully or be attuned to the other person's needs is not as strong. This leads easily to misunderstanding, often because one or both partners just doesn't listen or listens only to the point of understanding what he or she wants to hear. The oneness of infatuation turns into an unpleasant environment of stress and conflict that may have begun innocently enough with a decreased lack of motivation. How does psychological courage play a role here? Catch yourself, take the chance of communicating about issues as they arise in a marriage, push yourself to listen carefully. Much of this is not courage but self-discipline and empathy. However, treating your spouse as kindly as you treat your friends may take courage in admitting your own weaknesses and in caring when it is so much easier and less threatening to just not care. Once infatuation is gone, the easy road is the road to boredom or the end of a relationship. As Fromm says many times, to do an art well requires practice and the art of loving requires the awareness, empathy and courage to practice it even when we don't feel like it.

THE INTERNAL REWARDS OF COURAGE

Consider the example of a highly intelligent seven-year-old child whom I wish to teach to play chess, although the child has no particular desire to learn the game. The child does however have a very strong desire for candy and little chance of obtaining it. I therefore tell the child that if the child will play chess with me once a week I will give the child 50 cents worth of candy; moreover I tell the child that I will always play in such a way that it will be difficult, but not impossible, for the child to win and that, if the child wins, the child will receive an extra 50 cents worth of candy. Thus motivated the child plays and plays to win. Notice however that, so long as it is the candy alone which provides the child with a good reason for playing chess, the child has no reason not to cheat and every reason to cheat, provided he or she can do so successfully. But, so we may hope, there will come a time when the child will find in those goods specific to chess, in the achievement of a certain highly particular kind of analytical skill, strategic imagination and competitive intensity, a new set of reasons, reasons now not just for winning on a particular occasion, but for trying to excel in whatever way the game of chess demands. Now if the child cheats, he or she will be defeating not me, but himself or herself.

Alasdair MacIntyre, *After Virtue*, 2nd edition, 188.

Almost every adult in the world regardless of language or culture has some idea what "cheating" means. It might involve a school setting, a work or team project, the status of a hunter or warrior, or the faithfulness of a marriage. In all cases it means taking credit for something a person does not deserve—the paper taken off the Internet, the name surreptitiously added to a successful project, the false claim of military prowess or hunting skill, the assumption of trust by the spouse of the adulterer. And in all cases the person who cheats gets (or seeks) some *external reward*—a grade, a salary raise, the praise of fellow tribal members, sex with a new partner while also having a naive spouse as a domestic aide.

At the same time almost every adult knows another type of reward—what is called the "internal good" of an act or the *internal reward*.[8] The paper that was so incredibly tough to write turns into something that the student is genuinely proud of. That engineering project Dave could have cheated on but didn't turns into a building of real beauty that he was part of creating. The praise of the tribe for the hunter's skill is deserved and provides the hunter with a lifetime of memories. The love and faithfulness of a spouse is real and the richness of mutual love and communication make for an intimacy that cannot be described in words. This section is about the external-internal reward distinction and how that distinction applies to psychological courage.

The Internal-External Distinction in Everyday Life

Studies indicate that, given a choice, people will prefer internal goods to external ones. For example, a sense of competence in doing a difficult task well is more important than an external reward and introduction of an external reward like money actually *decreases* the enjoyment of the task.[9] However, in order to obtain the internal rewards of what we do in life, there is a catch. The joy of being competent is not achieved without hard work and honesty in the project. In other words, acting virtuously is a necessity. The virtues will differ according to the action but, without the relevant virtues, the internal rewards will not occur. In writing a paper, self-discipline, honesty, and perseverance are important. In hunting or in the military, courage, loyalty and reliability may be central. In a marriage, sensitivity, empathy and tact are critical. Getting the external reward—the grade, the trophy or the praise—may in fact require no virtues at all. Dishonesty, cowardice or greed may pay off handsomely. But internal rewards cannot be achieved without the relevant virtues.

We experience this distinction on a regular basis. For example, parents constantly run into it when raising children. A conversation with a child about her behavior can have as its main focus an external good or *ulterior motive* (e.g., what will the neighbors think or how will the child's behavior reflect on the parent's image) or an internal good (e.g., how can this conversation best help my child's psychological development). If the ulterior motive is truly the main goal of the conversation, then the parent may be teaching her child simply how to act to look good in which case virtues are irrelevant and vice may be useful. Children pick up on dishonesty quickly and soon understand the conversation is really about external goods and appearance. If parents play this game of hidden motives long enough, a child may come to think that all conversations have hidden ego-centered agendas. But if a parent has the child's own good in mind, the conversation must be honest and must have genuine empathy for the child. A genuine conversation has its own internal rewards which are long-lasting and often very enriching. But that does not happen without truthfulness and real caring for the child's development. Given a childhood filled with honest and loving interaction, a child can grow into an adult who does not need to deceive herself and who can have a sense of inner integrity in her various dealings in life. We recognize such people with integrity when they are adults; most begin with the simple everyday internal goods of honest and loving interaction with parents.

Other examples of the internal-external distinction are common. Young people with poor or average athletic ability may never win external rewards in a sport but the joy of the game can be theirs if they play the game with honesty and perseverance. If a school or parent puts all the emphasis on the external good like a trophy, the joy of the sport may be lost to the child. Businesses are by nature concerned about external rewards—profit is the bottom line. But owners and managers can vary enormously in how they structure the work environment. In some businesses employees are numbers; all interactions, even social ones, have some ulterior motive. Appearances are everything and there are few if any internal rewards to the job. Without the external reward of the paycheck no one would work there. But in other businesses employees are valued as real people and internal rewards can be high. Honesty dominates, loyalty counts, openness is encouraged and hard work is rewarded not *just* with the check but with a cooperative appreciation that makes working there a worthwhile part of a person's life. The family and the business world are worth comparing. For a family, when external rewards dominate the relationship, it is tragic because it can destroy what should be the deepest rewards in a child's life. A business, on the other hand, must have profitability at some level as a goal. Yet, even here an emphasis on the internal goods and the relevant virtues can make a profound difference in the quality of the experience.

Focusing on internal goods is a struggle in this society which daily preaches at us the idea that external goods are what really count. I am constantly struck by the number of students who think that almost all human practices have underlying ulterior motives. It is not hard to see why this attitude develops. Christmas, when sensitivity and caring are supposedly the virtues behind the practice, is instead a season of greed and how much money or material goods change hands. We become cynics easily. Similarly, sports have become a matter of money and status. The integrity of many sports is in serious question because, with the focus on external goods, honesty in the game can actually become a negative factor. Talk about "character building" rings hollow. Male-female relations have often become simply covers for sexual goals with television constantly portraying sex as the ulterior motive in relationships. The result, as some of my students tragically convey, is a loss of trust in which genuine relationships are impossible to form because of trying to determine or manipulate ulterior motives. The problem of the importance of external rewards is one with which Aristotle was familiar and his own answer varies at times. Sometimes he says external goods are a necessary complement to human happiness; at other times he implies the virtuous person has less need of them. Perhaps the middle road can help. Sports, conversations, family and job interactions all have external factors necessarily impinging upon them. Nothing is wrong with giving a trophy to a winner or discussing with a child society's expectations. The problem comes when the balance between the internal rewards and the external ones in the practice becomes distorted, e.g. when the trophy becomes all-important or when society's expectations become so dominant that they disrupt an otherwise honest interchange between parent and child. When that happens, human actions can become jaded to the point where, for example, some adults have little or no idea what a truly honest relationship is like. They are habituated to ulterior motives. We enrich our children's lives immeasurably by helping them to form habits of working for the internal rewards in life.

Before discussing specifically the internal goods of psychological courage, it is worth noting one final everyday example experienced by most citizens in Western society—the teacher-student relationship. This has relevance for all levels of teaching and for all types of teaching. What are the external rewards for the teacher? The major one in our culture is the paycheck but others might be status, honors or a certain appearance or image a person wants to project. What are the external rewards for students? The major one is the class grade but others include honors and, certainly, the monetary results of education. If internal goods are ignored, what will teachers and students do to achieve the external ones? A teacher may appear everyday and "go through the motions," whether it be reading notes to a college class or "sitting" on a group of third graders. Similarly, students will do what is necessary with the least amount of effort to get the external good; that might involve plagiarism, not doing assignments, or "working" a teacher for a grade to meet the criteria for a scholarship. For some college students the whole point is to get through with as least amount of effort as possible to get the grades, the degree, and eventually the money.

Now, no question, teachers need to earn what they deserve in educating the future of our society. Moreover, honors are important motivators for both teachers and students and the practical results of education for students are critical. Nevertheless, the teacher-student relationship provides one of the richest grounds available for internal rewards on both sides. The third grade teacher must work to eat but what she will remember is the student whose life she changed at a point where a young life is most vulnerable. The college professor may have his name in the paper but the heart of college teaching is the moment of understanding in the students' eyes and the recognition of the joy of learning that different classes can bring. The student may need the grade but what students remember as life-enhancing are certain projects or assignments, certain teachers who cared enough to communicate well and who loved their work, teachers who connected with the class. These internal goods of the teacher-student relationship are not achieved without certain fundamental virtues—conscientiousness, honesty, empathy, hard work. In the best of all possible worlds, the internal and external goods can be combined seamlessly. But for many human practices we must make a choice, sometimes small (what is really the point of this conversation), sometimes large (what career will I pick). Choices made for internal goods require virtues and, as crazy as it sounds today, virtue leads to happiness.

Psychological Courage and Internal Rewards

Running away from or giving in to our psychological fears can have short-term rewards. For example, as most smokers know, giving in to the addiction can provide a short-term relief of anxiety. The brain is briefly flooded with pleasure-inducing and calm-enhancing chemicals. But soon that passes, anxiety or the addictive need returns, and the process repeats itself. Likewise, the phobic who gets relief by avoiding high buildings, the obsessive-compulsive who follows the proper rituals, the self-deceptive person who achieves some temporary mental balance by avoiding the truth—all seem to be gaining some form of "good." In one sense, all those goods are "internal." Then how is the distinction between external and internal goods relevant here?

All the short-term benefits of giving in to psychological fears depend on some perceived need that in some way takes control of the person. *The need is experienced as "external" to our free choice, as forcing us to act.* Giving in to the fear gives temporary relief by allowing that demand to be satisfied for the time being. Such "external" demands have an obsessive character about them. The smoker *requires* the cigarette, the phobic *must* avoid high places, the obsessive-compulsive *must* follow the ritual and the self-deceptive person thinks he *cannot* face the truth. In a similar way, the athlete who *must* win the trophy at all cost may care little for how that is achieved and the student who *must* get the grade above all else will cheat if possible. What they all share, from the trophy to the cigarette to the ritual, is that the externally experienced demand on our life becomes the driving force behind the action. The key is the obsessive factor and the fear that provokes. As noted, trophies and money are great, but when they become an obsessive focus, virtue becomes irrelevant and the joys of internal rewards can easily get lost. Similarly, acts like smoking that relieve anxiety can be helpful in life, high places do require caution and some truth can be highly disturbing. But when the external factor—the cigarette, the building, the unpleasant truth—becomes the dominant focus of action and generates addictions, obsessions and fear, then the internal joys of life can be easily destroyed. Our life is no longer ours.

Self-deception, discussed at length in chapter one, also shows us a clear example of how lack of psychological courage can block the internal rewards of life. The philosopher Herbert Fingarette discusses the case of a mother who refuses to recognize the strong evidence that her son is delinquent and convinces herself that her son is a good boy.[10] What internal goods are being blocked here? A parent can relate to her child at many different levels. Some of the internal rewards of parenting are sharing new experiences with children, developing friendships with older children, and the sense of peace and comfort that arises from mutual trust. Child psychology books are filled with the internal rewards for the child of an honest and loving parent-child relationship. Self-deception regarding the nature of a child's actions means that, whenever that topic arises in consciousness or in conversation with the child or with others, falsity necessarily enters the picture. Experiences are not shared, friendship becomes a matter of manipulation, and trust is abused. In Fingarette's example the external goods are the need by the mother to maintain an emotionally comforting image of her son and (possibly) the need by the son to keep his mother self-deceived so that she does not get in his way. Self-deception automatically puts the focus of the mind on something other than the internal goods built into the nature of the relationship.

A similar example is given by the philosopher Bela Szabados who argues that self-deception may actually be a sign of internal goods. Szabados gives the example of a mother whose son is in a car accident.[11] It is not certain whether the child has been killed but the evidence strongly implies it. However, the mother refuses to believe the evidence until it conclusively proves her son is dead. Szabados argues that failure to deceive herself in this situation would indicate a lack of love for her son. Courage in facing the truth at all costs could actually *block* values like kindness, sympathy, and love.

But is this true? Is giving in to fear by the mother in this case a sign of love for her son and would facing the truth be a sign of callousness? This is what philosophers call a false dilemma. There is not a mutually exclusive relationship between accepting evidence and deep personal feelings; it is not *necessary* that a mother avoid negative evidence about her son in order to express deep love for him. Deep attachment is not easily broken but it is one thing not to want to accept the evidence and another thing not to accept it. Love in the example given would lead one not to want to accept the evidence but one could still accept it and grieve with as deep or deeper a sense of tragic loss as the mother who actually deceives herself. The mother might still have a slight hope that the evidence was wrong until proven conclusively. But hope is not self-deception. We can understand and sympathize with actual self-deception in this case but such examples do not supply evidence for a mutually exclusive relationship between truth and other human feelings.

A big difference exists between wanting to give in to a fear or harmful desire and actually doing that. The smoker may strongly want to continue but actions are what count. Or a person may want to preserve his social image by lying and hypocrisy but his actions will ultimately form his character. At various times we all will want an external or short-term good at all costs, but how we ultimately act on that determines whether psychological courage becomes a fact of life. In the case of the grieving mother a tendency to disbelieve the evidence is not in itself a vice. The test of a belief or feeling is in action and what makes self-deception a vice is what it does to the internal goods of life. Imagine that the mother in Szabados' example carries through into practice her desire to disbelieve the evidence and continues for some time to do that. What happens in her life? Honest conversation with doctors and relatives over the issue becomes skewed and distorted. Moreover, as discussed earlier in the book, denial may be a natural tendency in the face of death but staying in denial and acting on it leads to an inability to deal realistically with decisions that must be made. When this type of self-deception becomes common over any length of time, the internal goods become lost in the obsessive need to hide the truth. While everyone can understand self-deception in the mother's case, psychological courage is what will eventually allow the mother to regain her life and the internal goods of what life holds for her. If her son does die, she may think there are no such goods anymore. In our darkest moments courage is taking the risk that life is still worth living.

One reason that self-deception blocks internal goods is that it prevents an accurate judgment of an individual's ability relative to the standard of the practice. What does that mean? An example will clarify this point. Another philosopher, Robert Audi, gives the example of a student (Tom) who convinces himself that his paper is first-rate despite evidence to the contrary.[12] Tom then proceeds to act in ways which continue to promote this image, including leaving the room "to get some air" when his paper is discussed. The result of this false conception of his abilities will be that Tom is preventing himself from experiencing the internal rewards that go into genuine creative writing. *Self-deception prevents an accurate recognition of the standard by which Tom can grow as a writer.* We need standards to challenge us and force us to improve. Alasdair MacIntyre notes that "we cannot be initiated into a practice without accepting the authority of the best standards realized so far."[13] This applies to human practices as diverse as auto racing and music appreciation. A novice at auto racing will never experience the internal rewards of the sport if he cannot accept his own weaknesses compared to the standards of the best drivers. Likewise, a husband or wife who cannot accept his or her weaknesses will not be open to growth toward a better marriage. Self-deception blocks this ability to accept weaknesses; it blocks us from accepting our incapacity to judge correctly and prevents us from learning.

Psychological courage thus brings internal rewards because it makes us the owner of our lives. The self-deceiver, the person driven around by obsessive anxiety over control or dependency, the individual who must preserve self-image at all costs, the addict—all have their lives controlled by external forces which promise a seductive short-term good. But to achieve that externally driven good we must alienate ourselves, harm ourselves, or live in fear most of our lives. Internal rewards, even simple ones, can give us a basis for joy and positive life-long memories. The child who works hard to make the first soccer goal of his life is rightfully proud; so too the student who comes to appreciate a new artist or composer, the wife who has, perhaps for the first time, a truly genuine conversation with her husband, and the architect whose creativity is realized in a building. All such internal goods require real virtues. We do not have to be students, athletes, architects or parents to experience the internal rewards of psychological courage. We simply need to take the risk of owning our own decisions and living a life free of alienation and self-deception. The rewards of such integrity touch every part of our lives and can radiate outward to those with whom we live.

The Narrative of Our Lives

Despite how some philosophers and psychologists in the past have analyzed human behavior, our life is not a disconnected series of acts or events. Discrete events take place in a context and that context is the story or narrative by which we conceptualize our lives. Put another way, when you or I think of our lives (e.g., husband, father, teacher) we do so in terms of a narrative, a story that makes some coherent sense.[14] In Ann's mind it is the story of her being a mother; in Carrie's mind it is the narrative of her life as a teacher. If the story of our life breaks down, isolated specific events become meaningless. The trip to work, exercising, lunch—as distinct events the best they do is fill time and it does not take much for a life of time-fillers to become depressing. To say it is "all meaningless" is basically to say that our "life" has become a string of things we do that are unconnected to any plot. The plot, the story, gives us hope, makes the past and future *count*, and connects our personal story into part of a larger cultural and historical story (e.g., what being an American means). The narrative of our life fills our actions with significance beyond the act itself. We are at our deepest roots story-telling creatures.

Obsessions, addictions, self-deception, constant anxiety over our image—all can undercut the narrative of our lives because we are forced by our psychological fears to allow other people or things to direct the story. Acts are forced on us that distort the story we truly want to live. Soon such acts motivated by fear become meaningless. The terrible realization of the time spent in obsessive acts or in mindlessly pleasing others is deeply depressing because the acts themselves are divorced from our life-narrative. Psychological courage enhances the quality of our life's narrative. I want to spell out a few of those enhancements.

First, psychological courage enhances the *good* of our narrative. A meaningful life-story is centered around one or several "goods." The goods for millions of people are centered on family, career, religion, culture. Developing and enhancing these goods adds to our life-story in the same way that a well-developed theme in a novel adds enormously to the credibility and power of the book. For Andrew an addiction is destroying the unity of his life and preventing him from being a good father. The acts he does in the grip of the addiction are outside the story-line of what he sees as the goods of his life. No matter how intense the pleasure of the moment, the addictive act is an isolating one and afterwards, when seen in the light of his life-narrative, deeply depressing. Isolated acts forced on us by addictions and anxiety are meaningless acts and the more of them there are, the more the whole story-line of our life begins to break down. Psychological courage can be a central factor in rejuvenating the good of Andrew's life-story. Once again his life can make sense. His life once again has a clear *telos*, that is, a goal or set of goals that makes everything else worthwhile. And it is the courage to deal with the addiction that lets him work toward and realize those goals.

Second, psychological courage can make a life-narrative more *interesting*. A phobia, an addiction or a slavish need to look good at all costs restricts people's options enormously. Instead of going to the concert, agoraphobic Rebecca must stay home. Instead of watching his son in his first soccer game, Russ, who had a bad day, is looking for the bottle. When the counselor talks about the need to work through his hostility toward his wife and explore new ways of dealing with the problem, Mike ignores it because, after all, he doesn't have a hostility problem. By being hedged in with psychological fears, our "life" becomes not only a series of anxiety driven, meaningless acts but incredibly boring. Psychological courage allows us to engage the world in a way in which we can continue to have new experiences. It makes the story of our lives more interesting not only to ourselves but to those with whom we interact. At the same time, the broader interests and new experiences expand the good of our life-narrative. Going to the concert reminds Rebecca how much she loves music and she decides to pursue that degree which she thought before was impossible for her. Dealing with his anger by communicating with his wife turns into a whole new series of events that Mike and his wife enjoy together. Overcoming his anxiety about his dependency on others, Steve decides to do something to improve the world and takes up the challenge of the Peace Corps. The world can be a beautiful as well as a harsh and cruel place; all kinds of scenarios are possible. But it is not until we are willing to take the risk to engage the world as it is that more interesting options even enter the picture for us.

Third, psychological courage helps us understand with greater accuracy the narrative of *other people's lives*. Our life-narrative is set in a framework of our culture's narrative. If that cultural story breaks down, it is virtually impossible to maintain the viability of our individual story. And if our own life-story is fractured by acts forced on us by anxiety or fear, it becomes increasingly difficult to "read" the life-story of those around us with any accuracy. The greater the fear, the more the reading lens is distorted. Angela's obsessive need to control situations leads her to view fellow workers as competitors and potential threats. When one of them indicates she would like to pursue a friendship, Angela sees it as a back-door way for the other person to gain the upper hand. Opening up is dangerous and means potential loss of control and the genuine offer of friendship is turned down. Martin's alcoholism leads to a paranoid view of his wife's intentions. The reality of his wife's life-narrative becomes irrelevant when Martin drinks. Everything is focused on his own semi-delusional fears and anxieties. Since she must be lovable at all costs, Virginia consistently misreads advice given her by friends and relatives. Genuine concern is taken as criticism and her relationships are filled with misunderstanding about what "love" means. The genuine love of others is not returned because it is distorted by the narcissistic obsession to be accepted. While it is certainly true that no one ever reads another's life-narrative perfectly, it is also true that we can share in each other's stories and, with empathy and openness, go a long way toward understanding the goals and goods of another's life. Without courage to face our own fears and anxieties, the joy of sharing a story with someone else becomes difficult if not impossible.

COURAGE AND FRIENDSHIP

> After this the next step will be to discuss friendship; for it is a kind of virtue, or implies virtue, and it is also most necessary for living. Nobody would choose to live without friends even if he had all the other good things. . . . Friends are indeed a help both to the young, in keeping them from mistakes; and to the old, in caring for them and doing for them what through frailty they cannot do for themselves; and to those in the prime of life, by enabling them to carry out fine achievements. . . . Between friends there is no need for justice, but people who are just still need the quality of friendship; and indeed friendliness is considered to be justice in the fullest sense. It is not only a necessary thing but a splendid one. We praise those who love their friends, and the possession of many friends is held to be one of the fine things of life.
>
> Aristotle, *Nicomachean Ethics*.
> translated by J.A.K. Thomson, revised by Hugh Tredennick, 258–59.

Contrary to Aristotle, there may be people whose life-narrative does not include friends and whose life may nevertheless be richly textured. Some may be dedicated to a cause or project greater than themselves. Some may be intensely creative or so dedicated to scholarly work that no room exists for friendship. Happiness is certainly possible without friends. However, for the vast majority of us, friends are a critical part of our lives. At their best friends nourish each other, are there for each other in times of crisis, and help make this world a more pleasant place to live. But making and maintaining friends is not always easy. In this section I want to discuss courage and the rewards of friendship—making friends, types of friends and the challenges of friendship. Aristotle, whose insightful analysis of friendship I will draw upon frequently, viewed friends as the single most important way for us to learn about ourselves and to grow as human beings. While this may be a slight exaggeration, the point is that friends are reflections for each other through life and the deeper the friend, the more we can learn from the mirror of friendship.

Courage and Making Friends

For many people friendship is a natural outgrowth of childhood experiences shared together; for others it may stem from a natural ease they have with other people. Courage is not particularly important in forming such friendships, though certainly other virtues like honesty and loyalty are critical. But for many people making friends is not easy. Huge numbers of people in one degree or another have a form of social phobia. As discussed in chapter two, the extreme forms of such phobias usually require professional help to work through. The fear and anxiety are intense often to the point of near paralysis. But many people have fears of other people that are less debilitating but still enough to keep them from making friends. Sometimes it is the fear of crowds or groups of people. Many people feel uncomfortable in such settings and avoid them if possible. That makes forming friendships difficult since it limits the number of people a person meets. For other people making friends is difficult because it means opening up and knowing that your own weaknesses will be exposed. Rather than *ever* do that, it is just much easier not to make friends. We can convince ourselves then that making friends is not worth it. Frank has fought an alcohol problem for years and is deeply embarrassed by his failures. He has no intention of "making public" his personal problems and fears that "friends" can't be trusted. It's better to go through life with sporadic social relationships only and keep pretty much to himself. It's his problem, nobody else's, and he doesn't need the complication of other people's involvement. Always known as a "loner," Frank will deal with his own life, thank you, and his life is nobody else's business. His somewhat arrogant attitude partly hides a real fear of exposing who he "really" is to another person. Rather than do that, he has settled on the motto: Life is individualistic and hard—people ought to solve their own problems.

Now the first question is: Does Frank really want friends? Do people who are insecure in groups or who fear self-exposure actually, deep-down, genuinely want an open relationship with another person? I think the answer is mixed. Some people who are afraid of self-exposure or afraid of other people may have other interests which are not just cover-ups for fear. The gifted pianist, writer or naturalist may be deeply involved in a satisfying project and does not need friendship *and* at the same time may also have some social fear. One aspect of their personality may cause or reinforce the other but the fact is that, on balance, the person may not want friends for genuine reasons and the fear of other people is not the major driving force. However, and I would venture to say this is more common, large numbers of people who fear other people or fear self-exposure actually long for an open, trusting relationship with another person. They know, in moments when they are not deceiving themselves, that they are lonely and desperate for the psychological healing that friendship can supply.

This is where psychological courage becomes a central virtue. For those with a fear of other people, it is necessary to "catch" those moments of fear, seek help if necessary, but in any case *act* against the fear. It may result in a series of difficult choices but keep the goal in mind and maintain both mental awareness and courage. Take necessary practical steps like learning the art of conversation or how to listen to other people. Those steps can help enormously. For the person afraid of self-exposure, real courage lies not in continuing to hide but to open up and be willing to stand by who you are or have been. Yes, there may well be rejection. But that is where courage is needed — to take the psychological pain that may result at times. No one of us is a saint and part of friendship is helping each other heal and flourish. No chance at all exists for finding the healing of friendship unless you risk opening yourself. The Stoic point is again relevant. You cannot control what other people think, say, or do. Why let a fear of what you cannot control take control of *your* life? If you truly desire friendship, have the courage to open up to that possibility. You are looking for a friend. If other people have a problem with your past, that is their problem.

Another common reason people fear the closeness of friendship is because they have been hurt severely in the past when they did open up. As noted, people afraid of self-exposure may be ashamed or embarrassed or hiding from the possible pain of rejection. But some people have been truly hurt by prior friends and the idea of opening up again is too painful to consider. This goes beyond the fears mentioned in the previous paragraph. In this case friendship was tried but the result was deep pain and suffering. The level of courage needed to open up again to another person is significantly greater for such people.

Gina had a close friendship with Tim. It wasn't what usually passes for a romantic relationship but it was a relationship where each could share what was happening in his or her life and they helped each other enormously. When Gina was struggling with school, Tim was there for her. She sometimes thinks she could not have made it through without his support. When Tim's parents got divorced, it was Gina whom he called for help and support. It was as if they were brother and sister yet they were not and that in itself made the friendship special. But one day, for reasons Gina still does not completely understand, Tim began backing away. He was always "too busy" when she wanted to talk. When she asked him to explain why he was becoming distant, he talked around the issue and, unlike in the past, never came to the point. Gina tried several times to renew the old ties between them but Tim kept putting her off. Eventually Gina knew it was over. Never, with anyone else, had she opened herself up so deeply. Now, with hardly a word of honest explanation, the person she trusted more than anyone else was gone; it was as if they had never known each other. She vowed she was never going to be hurt like that again. Her life habits changed; when someone did make overtures of friendship, she immediately closed herself off. That pain was *not* going to be relived. Gina became a successful person in society's terms but she lived a life without friends, a life of continual self-protection.

This story, which at times sounds like a soap opera, is, I believe, very common. In one form of another millions of people have been abandoned by trusted friends. It may be in a marriage; it may be a childhood friend of many years; it may be the one person in your life that you finally came to trust. In all cases the breaking of trust is like tearing a portion of your self away; it is a ripping apart of your psyche. A hole is formed in your life and the vacuum left hurts incredibly. But in all cases the person must ask herself: what will I do now? You do have a choice. If you choose not to open up again, recognize clearly for yourself what a life without deep friendship will be like. Is that truly how you want to live your life? You may answer "yes" but know as fully as possible what you are doing. If you do want to experience again the joys of friendship, realize the courage it will take to open up again. The richness of friendship does not come cheap, the risk is proportionate to the reward. Facing that risk after being hurt may be one of the greatest acts of psychological courage you or I will ever have to do in our lives.

The Types of Friendship

We use the word "friend" very loosely in Western society. Someone we barely know may be "a friend I just met" or a speaker may begin an address with "Friends." Some people draw a distinction between "acquaintances" and "friends." Given the complexity of human relationships it is not surprising that the term is a slippery one. One of the oldest and still most viable ways to distinguish types of friends was the framework established by Aristotle. While it is also imperfect, it continues to be a useful way of analyzing what a "friend" is. His analysis also helps to clarify what courage has to do with friendship. Aristotle argues that there are three fundamental types of friends.[15] In this section I want to talk about the first two and reserve the third for the next section.

First are friends for utility or usefulness. Consider two examples. Julie becomes part of a joint project at work that will take some time. In the course of the project she finds she really enjoys working with Pam. They live a long away from each other and have very different social interests. Nevertheless, they work well together and their part of the project is going smoothly partly *because* they enjoy working together. This is a simple example of a friend for utility in which two or more people work together on some common project and come to enjoy each other's company. Julie would not say Pam is a close friend and the depth of their relationship extends only to the project they are working on. Nevertheless, Aristotle argues, it would be perfectly accurate for Julie to call Pam a "friend."

Friends for utility can come in many varieties. A customer-business relationship can develop into a utility friendship in which the customer consistently goes back to that particular store not just because of the product or service but because of one or more individuals working there. A taxi driver or bartender may develop utility friendships with certain customers. Clearly time spent together is relevant here. Aristotle and most people today would not call someone a "friend" if you worked with someone for ten minutes and never saw him again, even if you did enjoy each other's company. Likewise, a nice chat with a taxi driver or a customer hardly constitutes a friendship. So time spent together on some issue of utility—work, school, some service provided—is critical. Note also that friends for utility usually are what we might call "shallow." Such friendships may never go beyond the demands of work, current events, the class assignments. Nevertheless, such relationships can still be called "friendships," limited but genuine.

Aside from the fears of forming friends discussed above, it would not seem that courage is a particularly important virtue in friendships for utility. However, it could be relevant in at least two ways. First, in some cases, it may be necessary for a person to admit he or she needs help in some utilitarian situation. This is tough to do when your self-image is tied up with being capable of doing something alone. Many friendships formed around usefulness will never occur if one or both parties do not admit help of some sort is needed. This is unfortunate because often utility friendships make some of the most boring parts of life much more interesting and enjoyable. Second, utility friends may at times have to be courageous together for some goal. This would likely involve moral courage or possibly physical courage. Julie and Pam discover that their project is going to severely pollute the lake near the plant. Together they may support each other in being courageous. Two soldiers who have formed a friendship strictly because they were thrown together into the same platoon may help each other in the face of death. So, on the one hand, utility friendships are "shallow" in the sense that only a limited part of our life is shared with each other. On the other hand, situations may arise where, together, mutually enforced courage may cause people to do some very profound acts even up to and including facing the risk of death.

Utility friendships may or may not remain at that level. Some may evolve into what Aristotle calls "friends for pleasure." (And, likewise, friends for pleasure may change into or involve utility.) What are "friends for pleasure?" They are simply people we enjoy being around socially; they may or may not be the same people we work with. Sometimes the division is not clear. For example, friends who enjoy each other's company at a bridge club may be there for the "project" but may not see each other otherwise. The "utility" (the game) is still for them an enjoyable project. How should this be classified? Despite such ambiguous situations, the chief difference between friends for utility and friends for pleasure is that friends for pleasure primarily enjoy each other's company without any ulterior agenda. In its purest form friends for pleasure simply enjoy being around each other—talking, walking, eating or drinking together. Each finds the other witty, interesting or a pleasant person to be around. You may not share with such a friend deep elements of your personal life but that does not make such friendships utilitarian. The relationship is for enjoyment in itself.

What does courage have to do with this, if anything? Utility friendships can be formed even if the person is afraid of making friends because the project at work or school may literally force people to work together. But friends for pleasure are not formed by some external goal. For people afraid of opening up to people, friends for pleasure require a greater degree of psychological courage. A timid, shy person may use the work environment as a way to justify to herself the need to open up somewhat to another person. But that same shy person has no crutch when it comes to friends for pleasure. Emily would love to talk more with Tom but cannot get herself to socialize with him outside of their joint project at work. He may well be open to being a social friend but Emily will never find out if she does not have the courage to take the risk. In this situation practical techniques may again be vitally important. Learning how to approach people—reading up on what sort of things to say, practicing them—all can help "build up" courage. But ultimately Emily must take the steps on her own or the chance for social friendship will pass.

At least one other situation with social friends can make courage important. Social friendships involve pleasures in life. To the ancient Greeks that often meant drinking wine together and talking. A particular virtue that Aristotle called temperance applies to pleasure. Temperance is the proper or reasonable amount of pleasure, e.g., how much to drink. (Temperance does not mean abstaining from pleasures as the term is often used today.) Now courage might apply in this way. Imagine Chris and Jason are socializing and drinking together and Jason will be driving home alone. Chris knows this. Does Chris have the guts to try to stop his friend from drinking too much? The friendship is not very deep and the fear is that, if Chris tries to block Jason's pleasure, he may break off the friendship. Put more generally, do friends for pleasure have the courage to help each other be temperate? This is a fairly common scenario. Again the courage involved is psychological; the fear is being left alone or looking stupid before some larger group or perhaps being reminded of your own failures to be temperate. Without overcoming those fears Chris is not doing his friend any good by allowing him to drive home drunk. Friends help each other flourish. Giving in to the fear of confronting intemperance in a friend may make *you* feel temporarily safe but it could kill your friend. Social friends, who are social friends only, often avoid "delicate" areas. But there are times when courage is needed to give any meaning at all to the term "friendship."

The role of sexuality among friends for pleasure has never been clearly discussed. It involves issues such as whether sex in itself moves a friendship past the social friendship stage toward what Aristotle calls "complete friendship" or whether sex can be viewed simply as another shared pleasure among other pleasures like eating, drinking, or conversing. Today many people at least act as if the latter were the case. Some television programs and movies imply that sex among social friends is just another shared experience, certainly more intense and more complex than other pleasures, but still simply another shared pleasure. Friends for pleasure as traditionally defined do not share a great deal of personal information; there are clear boundaries between the deeply personal and the socially enjoyable. The question, and I simply raise it here for the reader's reflection, is whether sex automatically breaches that boundary. Are we kidding ourselves when we say sex can be simply a social experience? (The male and female perspectives may be quite different.) Do we, regardless of our gender, turn a social friendship into something else entirely when sex becomes involved or is it possible, as it may well be, for many people to isolate sex as simply another pleasure and to mutually agree that, like drinking, eating or talking, sex can be shared with no deeper implications? Certain courageous decisions must be made about choosing or not choosing to be sexual in a relationship. Clearly, for many, having sex with someone, especially a friend, moves the friendship beyond social toward what Aristotle called "complete friendship."

Complete Friends

The openness and trust of sexuality between friends ties into what Aristotle considers the highest and deepest form of human friendship, "perfect friends" or, I believe a better translation, "complete friends."[16] Complete friendship requires courage in a way friends for utility and pleasure do not. A complete friend is someone you can be completely trusting with, who is willing to share your life and you reciprocate. The ideal of complete friendship is total openness so that each person can help the other flourish in life. As a complete friend you care for the other because of who he or she is, not what he or she can do for you. Aristotle's term is also sometimes translated as "friends for virtue." Basically, through openness and sharing their deepest joys and fears and by being there for each other, complete friends help each other develop as human beings.

Our fast-paced highly mobile society makes such a deep friendship difficult to form and maintain. The constant barrage of "pleasure now" makes sacrifice, loyalty and openness appear to be a waste of time. Many view total openness with another person as stupidity—why open yourself to such a risk? And, even when friendship does approach this ideal, it requires constant awareness and a level of empathy that is virtually impossible to maintain.

But the rewards of such a friendship are profound. We cease to be emotional islands and for moments in our life we can completely relax without fear in the presence of another person. We spend vast amounts of energy guarding our personal borders in life. Friends for utility and pleasure allow us to loosen those guards to some degree. The loss of defensiveness and the shared moments together are why we enjoy such friendships. But complete friends are more than temporary. We know that they are always there for us and we are there for them. That awareness lets us go through life with greater serenity and emotional stability. Complete friendship is a rock on which the rest of our life can rest.

Ancient Greek society was strongly sexist and, unfortunately, Aristotle's writings are no exception. Nevertheless, he argues that a complete friendship based on the mutual goodness of both parties represents an ideal in a marriage.[17] Today this continues to be a relevant issue. Would you want to be in a marriage in which you and your spouse were not complete friends? In such a situation you would not (or rarely) share your life experiences together; you would not be there for each other emotionally. Marriages based primarily on utility reasons (e.g., money) or pleasure reasons (e.g., good sex or good times socially) are grounded on factors that have a transient characteristic. Times of crisis or emotional difficulty will cut into the utility or pleasure aspects of a marriage and then the question arises: Why are you together? The openness of complete friendship allows a couple to continue to accept the other person and work through together the times of crisis.

Another issue arises concerning friendship and marriage. Could you live with a situation in which your spouse was a complete friend with someone other than you? I have had married students tell me that they were not complete friends with their spouse. Some said that they did have such a friendship with someone else. In our society I think it is quite common for a male or female to have a complete friend of the same sex outside of marriage. A larger problem of course is when the complete friend is of the opposite sex. Since such friendship involves total openness and trust, it can easily lead into sexual relations (or sex can lead into complete friendship.) But then what is marriage about? Why be married when a spouse is a complete friend with somebody else, especially somebody of the opposite sex? I suspect millions of men and women accept the fact that their spouse is a deeper friend with someone of the same sex. A woman may feel she can be much freer to speak and be emotionally open with her female friend than with her husband. But when someone of the opposite sex is involved, a deep sense of betrayal can set in. The institution of marriage demands a certain amount of openness simply for people to live and function together. When a husband shares important parts of his life with a same sex friend the spouse can "compartmentalize" that. Males and females often have different interests. But when that sharing occurs with someone of the opposite sex, the entire framework of the marriage is cast into doubt because the kinds of things shared (including possibly sex) are exactly the kinds of things uniquely shared by the marriage partner. Such extra-marital complete friendships are extremely difficult to compartmentalize. So, prior to marriage, it is critical to ask yourself: Can I be a complete friend with this person and am I willing to work to make this friendship deeper and long-lasting? That question about friendship is in many ways as fundamental a question as the marriage vows themselves. The vows are public statements about what people must decide in private about the level of friendship they are choosing to enter.

What does courage have to do with complete friendship? A great deal but let's focus on three factors. First is the courage to open up and share your life. As noted earlier in the book, to do this is very threatening because we fear our "self" will be disturbed or shaken. Yes, in fact that might be true. But that is how people grow and flourish, not by hiding in a shell. A second factor in psychological courage is trusting the other person. Again, I discussed this earlier but it applies directly to complete friendship. Do you have the courage to trust the other person? That is why getting to know the other person is so important. Trusting out of desperation is much more likely to be rashness than courage. Trusting out of knowledge will still take courage but it is much more rational. So psychological courage in complete friendship is needed to risk opening yourself and to risk trusting the other person.

But a third factor in complete friendship also requires courage. I have had students argue that there is no such thing as a complete friend. All friendships are actually for utility or pleasure and what passes for complete friendship is just a sophisticated form of being self-centered and self-concerned. So the larger issue of courage is this. Are you willing to develop a friendship and live by the belief that a complete friendship is *possible*? A certain cynicism pervades Western culture about motives. Is it possible to truly put yourself in another person's shoes? Can you actually forget about yourself to care primarily about the needs of another person? Is the shared openness of complete friendship a truly unique experience? Aristotle would answer yes to all three questions but those are intellectual answers. In practice it takes courage for any of us to put into practice what we believe about the potential of a relationship. Courage in friendship is essential to open up the self and trust someone else; however, we also need first the courage to act on the belief that such a relationship is possible. Many people do not get past this point.

Challenges to Friendship

Friendship, even complete friendship, is never static. Besides the courage to make friends and to be open and trusting in a friendship, other challenges face friends simply because our lives are changing. In this final section on friendship I want to mention some challenges to complete friends and how psychological courage is helpful in dealing with them.

The first problem arises when one of the friends changes, especially in a direction that is harmful to himself or the friendship.[18] John and Mark have been close friends for years. They started out simply enjoying each other's company on the softball team but over time they have come to trust one another deeply. Each would say that the other is the most trustworthy and dependable person he knows. Mark begins to notice that John is drinking more than he ever did in the past. John admits it is because of his job; he desperately needs the job but the pressure is really getting to him. Despite his best efforts, Mark seems unable to stop what looks like a downward cycle for his friend. Aristotle argues that a complete friend has a duty to stick by and help his friend until it reaches a point where nothing can be done or it begins to seriously damage the character or personality of the person trying to help. John begins to break trust with Mark; during his drinking bouts he gossips about events and experiences that were privately told to him by Mark and he seems to be losing any ability to listen to Mark's point of view. How long should Mark stay and work on this friendship?

The scenario is a personal tragedy for both people because complete friendship is a rare and precious commodity. To follow Aristotle's advice Mark should work with John and try to help him as long as possible. He owes that to his friend. The length of time involved is not subject to some mathematical formula. True caring for a deep friend means having the courage to face some difficult circumstances, e.g., being able to take the abuse of trust which John displays and to keep caring for him. But at some point courage on Mark's part may become exploitation by John. Courage becomes rashness. Because Mark also has a duty to care about himself, not in a superficial way but as a flourishing human being, continuing to care in the face of an ongoing destructive response can eat away at Mark's own mental stability. It may reach a point where courage does not lie in continuing to trust and be open; the courage may lie in the gut-wrenching decision to end the friendship. None of this can be dictated by a third party or laid out with some rule. Counseling certainly would help. But the decision of where courage or cowardice begins in maintaining the friendship is a deeply personal decision. Changes in close friends present shifting boundaries of what is the best way to respond. Courage is involved in both choosing to continue to care in the face of apparent abuse of trust *and* in the decision to end the friendship.

A second issue raised by Aristotle is the number of complete friends that are possible for one person to have.[19] He himself argues for very few, most likely one. Though he does not spell it out in great detail, it clearly has to do with time and energy. A deep and close friendship requires spending time together and the energy involved in maintaining the friendship can be substantial. It certainly makes sense that one such friendship is the most realistic number. But I have had students who have argued that they have several complete friends and the reason is something Aristotle never foresaw — vast changes in communication technology. Students have claimed that they maintain complete friendship with several people through regular contact by phone or e-mail. There is a type of "conservation of energy" principle going on here. The friendships are completely open and life-sharing but the energy that goes into them is very focused and time-intensive. So, unlike the ancient Greeks, we do not leisurely meet with our friend in the marketplace to discuss our lives over wine. Instead, we limit our conversation to specific times and, when there, focus our energy more tightly on the conversation. Some students have argued that it is possible nowadays to have numerous complete friends because we do not have to be there physically in order to relate to them.

I take issue with this on two counts. First, there is more to being "present" to a person than simply the exchange of words. Granted, conversation is critical to complete friendship. It is the major form of shared communication. But it is not the only way. No amount of "emoticons" in an e-mail can make up for the bodily presence of another person. Body language, facial expressions, eye movements, tone of voice, or the touching of the other person can make all the difference between a "truthful" response to another person and a hollow response. While words open up our lives to one another, they are also the easiest vehicle of communication to hide behind. Complete friends recognize subtle changes in each other; they help each other flourish by having a depth of understanding lacking in friends for utility or pleasure. It is conceivable that technology down the road could break many of these barriers. A real-time hologram of your friend would do a lot. But physical touch and subtle emotional responses seem to require the physical presence of a friend.

Another problem with multiple complete friends is that such a friendship is grounded on total openness and the possibility of a conflict of interest is very real. If Jane is complete friends with Sarah and with Amy but Sarah and Amy are not complete friends, what does total openness mean in such a friendship? Jane's deep relationship with Sarah is certainly relevant to her relationship with Amy and vice-versa, so how much of that relationship with Sarah is shared with Amy, especially if Sarah and Amy are themselves not complete friends? This problem grows exponentially the more complete friends an individual has. A couple solutions may be possible. In an ideal situation Sarah and Amy would also be complete friends. Total openness between three or more people certainly is possible, though the changes in life-experiences each person would undergo would seem to make such a larger network of friendship fragile. Another solution, and probably more realistic, is that each of Jane's complete friends recognizes and respects her privacy as related to the other. Because both care for Jane, they do not put her into difficult or embarrassing situations. If Sarah started asking Jane invasive questions about her relationship with Amy, it might well indicate that Sarah is more interested in gossip or has succumbed to jealousy and has ceased to care about Jane's well-being. Complete friends respect each other's privacy. However, it is, I believe, a rare multiple friendship that can carry this off. Jealousy, mistrust, a sense of time lost with each other—any number of problems linger nearby. So Aristotle is probably right. Complete friendship is rare enough and maintaining one complete friendship can be a life-long task. With the time and energy involved and with the possible conflicts of interest, multiple complete friends, while not impossible, would be difficult to maintain over any length of time.

What does psychological courage have to do with multiple deep friendships? The issues raised earlier are all still present—overcoming the fear of opening up and trusting the other person. The latter is complicated by the fact that multiple friends put the issue of trust into the hands of more people. What may be a courageous act of trust with one person could be a rash act at times with multiple friends. I suspect the biggest role of courage in multiple friendships involves imposing or enforcing conversation limits that may harm your relationship with one of the other friends or be unjust to the other person in some way. At times in a two-way friendship it will take courage to tell someone you completely trust that you may *not* be ready or able to talk right now. It might imply a weakness in the friendship that probably is not there but which could lead to misunderstanding. While two friends can overcome that easily enough, with multiple friends, putting limits on a conversation because of the privacy needs of someone else will be much more difficult. Fears about misunderstanding and a perception of lack of openness are more likely because we are talking about someone other than the person you are talking to. There may be many more moments of fear and indecision with multiple friendships. Finding the mean in courage in this situation can be challenging to say the least. In the best of all possible worlds, multiple complete friends are so in balance with each other that no such fears exist. But in the real world of multiple friends moments of choice involving psychological courage are quite common.

Many other fascinating questions about complete friendship have been raised. Just to mention a couple. Can you be complete friends with your parents? (Would you willing to share problems with your sex life with your parents and vice-versa?) Must complete friendship be two-sided? For example, a deep long-term relationship with a counselor is almost certainly very one-sided yet has many elements of complete friendship. Would it be accurate to call the counselor a "friend?" While some of these issues might be semantic, whom we do or do not call a friend, especially a complete friend, is critical in most of our lives. The decision to be honest, open and trusting is a major issue of courage in life and how we do that and with whom are central to the quality of our time on earth.

PSYCHOLOGICAL COURAGE
AND THE REWARDS FOR SOCIETY

As thefts increase, and the stolen goods are seen, heard about, or even smelled in the rest of the camp, inevitably rumors start to circulate. One hears that meat is disappearing "regularly" from the butchery, potatoes from the vegetable tables, and coal from the piles. Other workers, hearing these reports of goods enjoyed at home, begin to lose interest in resisting their own forms of the same sort of temptation. As a helper in the kitchen said once to Stan, "If all these other guys are taking stuff home to their kids, why the hell should mine go hungry? I'm going to get in on this before it's all gone!"

The virus spreads. Twenty-five pounds of meat stolen grow to fifty, and then to a hundred, and pretty soon the diners are getting noticeably less than their fair share of the issued supplies. . . .

Men who had worked for a considerable period as cooks in the kitchen and seemed happy on the job would ask to be transferred. When Matt wanted to know why, their answer would go something like this:

"The kitchen isn't what it used to be. Everybody is suspicious of everybody else. Most of all, the people suspect me, the cook. I'm supposed to be responsible for my shift—that means for the honesty of my crew. I don't know if they're taking stuff behind my back or not—probably a little, but I have no idea how much. If they're taking a lot, then we're a bunch of phonies, pretending to feed the diners but actually feeding ourselves. . . ."

"Yes, and that's not all," said Matt. . . . "You can see what is happening. As the honest chaps get uneasy and want to move out, the scroungers move up—up from the ranks of helper and right into the heart of the organization itself, to cook if Brockman quits and, brother, if you quit and no one else will do it, they'll move right into manager, too. Then the disease will have killed the patient, and the kitchen as a means of feeding the diners will have died. Immorality, my friend, is not merely the private demon of the 'missionary saints'. . . . It's more like a public demon, and it can bring a society to its knees as surely as any physical plague!"

Langdon Gilkey, *Shantung Compound*, 148–49.

The Radiating Effect of Psychological Problems

I want to start with a claim that seems self-evident. A person's psychological problems—anxieties, obsessions, phobias, depression—affect the people around them. This fact is not only intuitively obvious but study after study shows the harmful effects of such problems on families and loved ones. However, my point in this section is to argue that, *far more than we realize*, the psychological problems of individuals affect society at large. Thus psychological courage in facing such problems not only can benefit the person and the immediate family but social institutions as a whole.

Everyone is aware of the fact that relationships in a workplace or in a setting like a school or church can be strained enormously by the obsessions or anxieties of one person. There are people no one wants to work with because of their anger problems, their irrational fears or hatred of certain groups, or their excessive shyness. Often, what others interpret as laziness may be a phobia. At work Nick is really upset at Michelle. She never contributes to the project and, though she seems capable enough, never is around to help when he needs her. She is often late for meetings and likes to sit near the back, never saying a word. What on earth is the matter with her? As noted in chapter three, we tend to attribute to other people motives that we are familiar with. Nick's only explanation that he can think of is that Michelle is just plain lazy and is looking for the paycheck without having to do her part. The truth, however, is quite different. Michelle has a severe social phobia. She is panic-stricken at the thought of speaking in public and is wary of strangers. She would like to contribute to the group project but in quiet, unobtrusive ways, but she hasn't found any way to do that yet. By being late to meetings she does not have to "happy talk" with anyone beforehand, a terrifying thought. She does not think her verbal contributions are worth much anyway and the thought of being criticized for her comments is too much to bear. It is not simply enough to tell her she needs to participate. Until she deals with her phobia she will not be a productive work colleague. Her phobia radiates outward to the whole group and a certain amount of cynicism about people "who don't pull their weight" permeates the project. The group leader has a much more difficult time not only because of Michelle but because of other people's reaction to her. No question, the company is suffering because of Michelle's lack of contributions but also, no question, Michelle is suffering inside for very personal reasons. Psychological courage combined with the techniques available to help with phobias would not only help Michelle but would make her workplace much more productive and enjoyable for all concerned.

Probably the most destructive radiating social effect of psychological problems involves the use and abuse of power. A good deal of speculation has gone on about how the psychological problems of people like Napoleon or Hitler drove them to do what they did. Historical events are almost always multi-causal so it is virtually impossible to pin down how much personal psychology was responsible for Hitler compared to the socio-cultural situation at the time in Germany. Nevertheless, it is clear that very often psychological fears or irrational motives on the part of those in power can be harmful and, at times, catastrophic for society at large.

A good example of this is the defense mechanism called projection. No matter how one interprets this strange phenomenon, it happens. Hostile people view the world as a dangerous place and in more extreme forms view individuals or groups in the world as out to get them. Here is at least one potential scenario. As a child Andrew bounced around from foster home to foster home. He never had anybody care about him very much and some people said he seemed to be hostile all the time. People made him angry easily and he never thought about what their situations might be like. As he got older, he gradually began to notice similarities between people that angered him. He noticed that certain groups of people seemed to get all the favors in society and people like him never got any. They were especially out to get guys like him who weren't "upper class" and who had to scratch for a living. He could easily see that one ethnic group especially seemed to have all the power and money. If it were not for them, his rotten existence would be better. Andrew joins an organization designed to bring down that group by whatever means. A new Klan member is born.

Granting the multi-causal factors involved, Andrew's irrational psychological state played a major role in his social actions—a strengthening of the Klan. The cause of his consistent hostility may be environmental, e.g., a total lack of affection and love as a child, or it may be genetic. It may be both, with a genetic tendency leading to people avoiding him which reinforced the personality trait, and so on. Regardless, Andrew "projects" his hatred into the world and the result is an irrational interpretation of what is happening around him, ranging from the "look" of another child on the playground to the "conspiracy" of some ethnic group. But imagine for a moment a flash of insight on Andrew's part—perhaps his little sister marries a member of that ethnic group and for a few moments Andrew questions his own judgment. Imagine further that, despite his web of social connections already in place and the time in his life already devoted to the cause of prejudice and hatred, Andrew takes that insight and acts on it—an act of deep and genuine courage in his case. Perhaps he makes a point of getting to know his brother-in-law better or decides to take seriously one of those "damn counselors" people pitched at him as a kid. Finally, imagine he begins to realize empathy for others and appreciate diversity in modern society. He breaks his ties to the Klan, the Klan becomes weaker without Andrew, and the fear level of the local community drops significantly. This sort of thing has happened. It represents a clear example of where a moment of psychological courage can profoundly affect the surrounding society. Personal problems projected onto others by leaders in power have, I would venture to say, caused untold millions to suffer and die in this world. An increase in psychological courage in dealing with personal psychological problems could benefit society enormously.

Projection is not the only defense mechanism with wide-ranging social effects. Displacement, or the transfer of impulses from threatening objects to less threatening objects, plays a role in both family and social violence. The classic example is the spouse, frustrated at work and unable to say or do anything to the boss, who comes home and takes it out on the other spouse, the children or the pet dog. This is sometimes treated lightly but consider in your own life how common it has been. Frustration is closely linked to aggression, both verbally and physically, and the level of domestic conflict, certainly in words and probably in actions, is higher because people displace their frustration onto the family or some ethnic group that will not fight back. Consider the social impact of psychological courage here in honestly facing the source of our emotional turmoil, in confronting in ourselves the true innocence of our victims, and in trying to get to the genuine root of the problem.

Other defense mechanisms, perhaps more controversial in the psychological community, could also be cited as causes for social disharmony. Reaction formation is one of those. A person assumes behavior opposite the feeling that is being repressed in order to keep the feeling out of consciousness. Some highly irrational actions can result. Compulsive crusaders against gays and lesbians may be covering up their own sexual tendencies which they cannot admit to themselves. Yet another defense mechanism, denial, discussed in chapter one under self-deception, is fundamental in allowing a person to harm others and then rationalizing the actions. All the defense mechanisms rely on running away from our own emotions; the harm society suffers is tied to a person with power of some kind being unable or unwilling to face his or her own weaknesses. Admitting to consciousness emotions like anger or frustration at least can make a person somewhat aware of when those emotions are expressed in the wrong place. Likewise, admitting and "owning" our own sexual tendencies or tendencies to cover up unpleasant truths is a major step toward eliminating denial and reaction formation. Behavioral psychologists are correct that much of the behavior discussed in this section can be understood by patterns of reinforcement and can be cured without the need for deep "insight" therapy. However, personal awareness and personal acceptance of what motivates us are steps for most people toward better adjustment to reality. It takes courage to face those fears and unpleasant facts and, even in behavioral therapy, it takes a certain degree of courage to enter therapy, continue it, and act on it. No matter how the problem is approached, without psychological courage, the radiating effect of our own personal problems will continue to have negative effects on the society around us. For those in power who are afraid to face their own weaknesses, that effect on society can be devastating.

The Effect of Virtue and Vice on Social Practices

Picture this: You are in a Japanese internment camp in China during the Second World War. The camp is about 200 yards wide at its widest point by 105 yards long at its longest and it has several buildings, mainly dormitory-type dwellings and kitchen facilities. You and a group composed mostly of strangers, up to 2000 altogether, are told to live in the camp. Very basic needs are supplied by the Japanese but, other than that, you are on your own. Make a life.

After the incredible difficulties of organizing living arrangements and work assignments, life becomes bearable under the conditions. Friendships are made and your "on-the-spot" society with people ranging from monks to sailors is functional. But then something curious happens. A few people start to "cheat." They take home extra food from the kitchen and lie about it. Pretty soon more and more people do it and the kitchen, which before had done a fine job of serving this tiny society, is becoming virtually impossible to run and maintain. Moreover, a few people get greedy and possessive. When a shipment of Red Cross packages arrives and a decision is made to distribute them evenly, some of the Americans in this multicultural group insist that, since it is the Americans that sent them, Americans should get total control of them. The entire process of distribution is sabotaged. What you are witnessing is a fact of human social life—the corrupting effect of vice on social institutions. This effect is as real as the lack of food, clothing and shelter and it can destroy the best of what humans have created.

The images in the above paragraph, taken from the remarkable autobiographical book by Langdon Gilkey, *Shantung Compound*, point to what may be the most significant effect of courage on society.[20] Virtues like honesty, courage, generosity, and self-discipline strengthen the traditions of which they are a part. Vices like dishonesty, cowardice, greed and laziness, while they may produce short-term benefits for the individual, eat away at the trust and cooperation required for us to live together. Virtues strengthen the bonds between us, whether it be in a game, a business, or a family. Vices can destroy those bonds.[21] A friendly game of baseball cannot be played if too many people cheat and a democratic government cannot function if people do not trust it. Without at least a reasonable degree of honesty a business could not function, no matter how many security cameras were focused on employees and customers. *Virtues are the glue that hold the social fabric together.* Without virtues external forces are necessary to maintain a facade of order. That order, whether it be a tyranny in government or a business, is a shell in which people live in fear, mistrust and resentment.

Courage is a critical virtue in maintaining and strengthening our life together. Sometimes, as in the physical courage displayed in the World Trade Center attack, it lights up for us the value we put on our life together and reminds us that some of us are willing to risk death for the sake of others. Such courage is an essential foundation for trust, especially in times of crisis. Other times, as in the moral courage of a Rosa Parks or some individuals discussed in *Shantung Compound*, courage strengthens the fabric of society by forcing us to look at weaknesses in our tradition—open wounds that we do not want to face. Still other times, as in the psychological courage of the addict facing alcoholism or a person dealing with agoraphobia, the individual becomes stronger, more trustworthy, more capable of giving and receiving love, more an integrated part of the fabric of society. All forms of courage promote a stronger society by increasing trust, confidence and a sense of well-being.

As noted above, the person who is psychologically afraid of facing her own emotions and fears, especially when in a position of power, will likely disrupt the tradition of which she is a part because her main concern is self-protection, not the greater good or the practice at hand. Psychological courage lays the groundwork for a society in which all members can participate *without* having ulterior motives based on personal fears. This very common but hidden phenomenon, acting with personal fears or addictions as ulterior motives while putting on a "proper" front to society, is one that not only leads to personal unhappiness and an emotional trap but prevents society from benefiting from the potential of each member. When combined with physical and moral courage, an increase in psychological courage gives not only the individual but all of society a genuine hope for a stronger future.

NOTES

1. Robert Baron and Donn Byrne, *Social Psychology: Understanding Human Interaction* (Boston: Allyn and Bacon, 1994), 336.

2. Baron and Byrne, *Social Psychology*, 337–38.

3. Erich Fromm, *The Art of Loving* (New York: Harper and Row, 1956).

4. Fromm, *Art of Loving*, 1–2.

5. Fromm, *Art of Loving*, 2–3.

6. Fromm, *Art of Loving*, 3–4.

7. See R.S. Miller, "On Decorum in Close Relationships: Why Aren't We Polite to Those We Love?" *Contemporary Social Psychology* 15 (1991): 63–65.

8. Alasdair MacIntyre, *After Virtue*, 2nd edition (Notre Dame: University of Notre Dame Press, 1984), 188–92.

9. Edward Deci, "Effects of Externally Mediated Rewards on Intrinsic Motivation," *Journal of Personality and Social Psychology* 18 (1971): 103–115; Mark Lepper and David Greene, "Undermining Children's Intrinsic Interest with Extrinsic Reward," *Journal of Personality and Social Psychology* 28 (1973): 129–37.

10. Herbert Fingarette, *Self-Deception* (London: Routledge and Kegan Paul, 1969), 18–20, 50–51.

11. Bela Szabados, "The Morality of Self-Deception," *Dialogue* 13 (1974): 29.

12. Robert Audi, "Self-Deception, Action and Will," *Erkenntnis* 18 (1982): 148–53.

13. MacIntyre, *After Virtue*, 190.

14. See MacIntyre, *After Virtue*, chapter 15.

15. Aristotle, *Nicomachean Ethics*, trans. S.A.K. Thomson, revised by Hugh Tredennick (London: Penguin Books, 1976), 261–64.

16. Aristotle, *Nicomachean Ethics*, 263–64. The phrase "complete friendship" in the *Nicomachean Ethics* is the translation of Terence Irwin (Indianapolis: Hackett Publishing Co., 1985).

17. Aristotle, *Ethics*, 280–81.

18. Aristotle, *Ethics*, 291–93.

19. Aristotle, *Ethics*, 307–8.

20. Langdon Gilkey, *Shantung Compound* (New York: Harper and Row, 1966).

21. MacIntyre, *After Virtue*, 195–203.

Bibliography

Aristotle. *Nicomachean Ethics*, trans. J.A.K. Thomson, revised Hugh Tredennick. London: Penguin Books, 1976.

——. *Nicomachean Ethics*, trans. Terence Irwin. Indianapolis: Hackett Publishing Co., 1985.

Aronson, Elliot. *The Social Animal*. 7th ed. New York: Freeman, 1995.

Audi, Robert. "Self-Deception, Action, and Will." *Erkenntnis* 18 (1982): 133–58.

——. "Self-Deception and Rationality." Pp. 169–94 in *Self-Deception and Self-Understanding*, edited by Mike W. Martin. Lawrence, Kansas: University Press of Kansas, 1985.

Babior, Shirley, and Carol Goldman. *Overcoming Panic, Anxiety and Phobias*. Duluth, Minnesota: Whole Person Associates, Inc., 1996.

Baron, Robert, and Donn Byrne. *Social Psychology: Understanding Human Interaction*. Boston: Allyn and Bacon, 1994.

Beck, Aaron, Arthur Freeman, and Associates. *Cognitive Therapy of Personality Disorders*. New York: The Guilford Press, 1990.

Beck, Charlotte Joko. *Everyday Zen: Love and Work*. New York: HarperCollins, 1989.

Callan, Eamonn. "Patience and Courage." *Philosophy* 68 (1993): 523–39.

Chödrön, Pema. *The Wisdom of No Escape and the Path of Loving-Kindness*. Boston: Shambhala Publications, 1991.

Confucius. *The Essential Confucius*, trans. Thomas Cleary. San Francisco: Harper San Francisco, 1992.

Darley, John, and Charles Batson. "From Jerusalem to Jericho: A Study of Situational and Dispositional Variables in Helping Behavior." *Journal of Personality and Social Psychology* 27 (1973); 100–8.

Davison, Gerald, and John Neale, *Abnormal Psychology*. Rev. 6th ed. New York: Wiley, 1996.

Deci, Edward. "Effects of Externally Mediated Rewards on Intrinsic Motivation." *Journal of Personality and Social Psychology* 18 (1971): 103–15.

Epictetus. *The Handbook of Epictetus*, trans. Nicholas White. Indianapolis: Hackett Publishing Co., 1983.

Festinger, Leon, Henry Riecken, and Stanley Schachter. *When Prophecy Fails*. New York: Harper Torchbooks, 1956.

Fingarette, Herbert. *Self-Deception*. London: Routledge and Kegan Paul, 1969.

Friese, Kay. "Rosa Parks." Pp. 489–92 in *The Book of Virtues*, edited by William Bennett. New York: Simon and Schuster, 1993.

Fromm, Erich. *The Art of Loving*. New York: Harper and Row, 1956.

Gilkey, Langdon. *Shantung Compound*. New York: Harper and Row, 1966.

Gilligan, Carol. *In a Different Voice: Psychological Theory and Women's Development*. Cambridge: Harvard University Press, 1982.

Goodwin, Donald. *Anxiety*. Oxford: Oxford University Press, 1986.

Holmes, David. *Abnormal Psychology*, 2nd ed. New York: HarperCollins, 1994.

Jones, Edward, and Keith Davis. "From Acts to Dispositions: The Attribution Process in Person Perception." Pp. 219–66 in *Advances in Experimental Social Psychology*, vol. 2, edited by L. Berkowitz. New York: Academic Press, 1965.

Jones, Edward, and Richard Nisbett. *The Actor and the Observer: Divergent Perceptions of the Causes of Behavior*. Morristown, New Jersey: General Learning Press, 1971.

Keen, Sam. *Gabriel Marcel*. Richmond, Virginia: John Knox Press, 1967.

Latané, Bibb, and John Darley. *The Unresponsive Bystander: Why Doesn't He Help?* New York: Appleton-Century-Crofts, 1970.

Lepper, Mark, and David Greene. "Undermining Children's Intrinsic Interest with Extrinsic Reward." *Journal of Personality and Social Psychology* 28 (1973): 129–37.

MacIntyre, Alasdair. *After Virtue*. 2nd ed. Notre Dame, Indiana: University of Notre Dame Press, 1984.

Marcel, Gabriel. *The Philosophy of Existentialism*. New York: Citadel Press, 1964.

Martin, Mike W. *Self-Deception and Morality*. Lawrence, Kansas: University Press of Kansas, 1986.

Meiland, J.W. "What Ought We to Believe? or The Ethics of Belief Revisited." *American Philosophical Quarterly* 17, no. 1 (January, 1980): 15–24.

Metzger, L. *From Denial to Recovery: Counseling Problem Drinkers, Alcoholics and their Families*. San Francisco: Jossey-Bass, 1988.

Milgram, Stanley. *Obedience to Authority*. New York: Harper, 1974.

Miller, R.S. "On Decorum in Close Relationships: Why Aren't We Polite to Those We Love?" *Contemporary Social Psychology* 15 (1991): 63–65.

Morris, Desmond. *The Naked Ape*. New York: McGraw-Hill, 1967.

Oltmanns, Thomas F., John M. Neale, and Gerald C. Davison. *Case Studies in Abnormal Psychology*. 4th ed. New York: Wiley, 1995.

Peck, M. Scott. *People of the Lie: the Hope for Healing Human Evil*. New York: Simon and Schuster, 1983.

Peterson, Christopher. *The Psychology of Abnormality*. New York: Harcourt Brace, 1996.

Peurifoy, Reneau. *Anxiety, Phobias, and Panic*. New York: Warner Books, 1995.

Plato. *The Apology.* Pp. 37–67 in *The Last Days of Socrates*, trans. Hugh Tredennick and Harold Tarrant. London: Penguin Books, 1993.

Putman, Daniel. "Virtue and Self-Deception." *Southern Journal of Philosophy* 25 (Winter, 1987): 549–57.

———. "Psychological Courage." *Philosophy, Psychiatry and Psychology* 4 (March, 1997): 1–11.

———. "The Emotions of Courage." *Journal of Social Philosophy* 32 (Winter, 2001): 463–70.

Reps, Paul, and Nyogen Senzaki, eds. *Zen Flesh, Zen Bones.* Boston: Shambhala Publications, 1994.

Rorty, Amelie. "Belief and Self-Deception." *Inquiry* 15 (1972): 387–410.

Ross, Nancy Wilson. *Buddhism: A Way of Life and Thought.* New York: Vintage Books, 1980.

Serignar, C.B. *From Panic to Peace of Mind.* Gretna, Louisiana: Wellness Institute, 1991.

Swift, Carolyn. "Surviving: Women's Strength through Connection." Pp. 153–69 in *Abuse and Victimization across the Life Span*, edited by M. Straus. Baltimore: Johns Hopkins, 1988.

Szabados, Bela. "The Morality of Self-Deception." *Dialogue* 13 (1974): 25–34.

———. "The Self, Its Passions and Self-Deception." Pp. 143–68 in *Self-Deception and Self-Understanding*, edited by Mike W. Martin. Lawrence, Kansas: University Press of Kansas, 1985.

Thich Nhat Hanh. *Peace is Every Step: The Path of Mindfulness in Everyday Life.* New York: Bantam, 1991.

U.S. News and World Report, October 1, 2001.

Vitkus, John. *Casebook in Abnormal Psychology.* 3rd ed. New York: McGraw-Hill, 1996.

Index

About the Author

Daniel Putman is Professor of Philosophy at the University of Wisconsin—Fox Valley. He is the author of *Human Excellence: Dialogues on Virtue Theory*, also published by UPA. In addition he is the author of over 25 articles on ethics and virtue theory in professional journals such as *Philosophy, Journal of Social Philosophy, American Philosophical Quarterly, Teaching Philosophy, Journal of Value Inquiry, Journal of Moral Education* and *Philosophy, Psychiatry and Psychology*.